The Struggle for the History of Education

The history of education is a contested field of study, and has represented a site of struggle for the past century of its development. It is highly relevant to an understanding of broader issues in history, education and society, and yet has often been regarded as being merely peripheral rather than central to them.

Over the years the history of education has passed through a number of approaches, more recently engaging with different areas such as curriculum, teaching and gender, although often losing sight of a common cause. In this book Gary McCulloch contextualizes the struggle for educational history, explaining and making suggestions for the future on a number of topics, including:

- finding a set of common causes for the field as a whole;
- engaging more effectively with social sciences and humanities while maintaining historical integrity;
- forming a rationale of missions and goals for the field;
- defining the overall content of the subject, its priorities and agendas;
- reassessing the relevance of educational history to current educational and social issues.

Throughout this book the origins of unresolved debates and tensions about the nature of the field of history of education are discussed and key examples are analysed to present a new view of future development.

The Struggle for the History of Education demonstrates the key changes and continuities in the field and its relationship with education, history and the social sciences over the past century. It also reveals how the history of education can build on an enhanced sense of its own past, and the common and integrating mission that makes it distinctive, interesting and important for a wide range of scholars from different backgrounds.

Gary McCulloch is the inaugural Brian Simon Professor of the History of Education at the Institute of Education, University of London, UK.

Foundations and Futures of Education

Series Editors:

Peter Aggleton, *School of Education and Social Work, University of Sussex, UK*
Sally Power, *Cardiff University, UK*
Michael Reiss, *Institute of Education, University of London, UK*

Foundations and Futures of Education focuses on key emerging issues in education as well as continuing debates within the field. The series is interdisciplinary, and includes historical, philosophical, sociological, psychological and comparative perspectives on three major themes: the purposes and nature of education; increasing interdisciplinarity within the subject; and the theory–practice divide.

Previous titles include:

Schools and Schooling in the Digital Age
Neil Selwyn

The Irregular School
Roger Slee

School Trouble
Deborah Youdell

Radical Education and the Common School
Michael Fielding and Peter Moss

The Struggle for the History of Education

Gary McCulloch

Routledge
Taylor & Francis Group

LONDON AND NEW YORK

First edition published 2011
by Routledge
2 Park Square, Milton Park, Abingdon, Oxon, OX14 4RN

Simultaneously published in the USA and Canada
by Routledge
270 Madison Avenue, New York, NY 10016

Routledge is an imprint of the Taylor & Francis Group, an informa business

British Library Cataloguing in Publication Data
A catalogue record for this book is available from the British Library.

Library of Congress Cataloging-in-Publication Data
McCulloch, Gary.
The struggle for the history of education/Gary McCulloch.—1st ed.
p. cm.
Includes bibliographical references.
1. Education—History. I. Title.
LA11.M36 2011
370.9—dc22
2010038939

ISBN13: 978–0–415–56534–9 (hbk)
ISBN13: 978–0–415–56535–6 (pbk)
ISBN13: 978–0–203–82885–4 (ebk)

Typeset in Garamond by Swales & Willis Ltd, Exeter, Devon

Printed and Bound in Great Britain by TJ International Ltd, Padstow, Cornwall

Contents

Acknowledgements

This book is an outcome of my teaching, research and discussions with colleagues and students about the history of education over more than a quarter of a century, and accordingly I have many debts to record; too many indeed to acknowledge properly in such a brief space. As will be evident, I have been an active protagonist in, as well as a keen observer of, debates around the history of education since the 1980s. This involvement may be traced in the many articles, conference papers, monographs and book reviews which I have written over this time. I am happy to acknowledge these earlier labours on my part, some of which are discussed and further rehearsed here.

I would like to thank all of my colleagues and students around the world who I have worked with, and also all those who have attended seminars and conferences and taken part with me in debates around the development of the field. I record also my debt to the many excellent historians of education who have inspired my own work and encouraged me to think about the aims and purposes of this area of study. My colleagues and students from my time at the University of Auckland in New Zealand from 1983 until 1991 played a key formative role in this process. I also appreciate the contributions of those at other universities where I have been based over the years, in particular, because most recent and most directly relevant to this current work, at the Institute of Education, University of London, where I have had the honour to be the Brian Simon Professor of the History of Education since 2003. I am also grateful to the archivists at the Institute of Education for their help in providing access to the papers of Fred Clarke and Brian Simon. The collegiality of conferences of history of education societies that I have experienced in England, the US, Australia, New Zealand and elsewhere is also very worthy of special mention.

Richard Aldrich, Clyde Chitty, Peter Cunningham, Tom O'Donoghue and Barry Franklin have kindly read and discussed chapters in this book. Michael Reiss, Peter Aggleton and Sally Power, as series editors, have given much valued advice and support. I am also grateful to Routledge, especially to Anna Clarkson, for their patience as I completed the book. My family, especially my wife Sarah, has, as always, given me unstinting support during the writing of this work, and I dedicate the book to my mother and the memory of my late father. As always, all shortcomings and the general responsibility for this book are my own.

Gary McCulloch

1 Introduction

History, education and the social sciences

The educational past might appear to be rather intellectual or academic, as opposed to being engaged in the battlefields of history where real blood is spilled. It might seem sedate when compared with the revolutionary struggles of the past. It could come across as being less inspiring than the great struggles for liberation, social justice and democracy. And yet the history of education is all about struggle. Education has been at the heart of all of the key struggles of modern times in different parts of the world. It has been a rallying call for social progress, change and equality, and has been fundamental to social class struggles, struggles for democracy, and the fight for social justice. Education has also been uppermost in personal success and failure, in triumph and defeat, and such struggles too have their history. We may pause to recall our own struggles with schools, teachers and examinations, or with learning in general at school, at university, or in everyday life, and then we can recognize that education is indeed a struggle, and always has been.

The study of the history of education is also a site of struggle. It is an exciting and intellectually challenging field of study that is highly relevant to an understanding of broader issues in history, education and society at large. At the same time, it is subject to often fierce debates and underlying uncertainties about its identity and its future direction as a field. It is riven by fissures and beset with insecurities. As Richard Aldrich has observed, it is, always has been, and always will be, a contested and changing terrain (Aldrich 2000, p. 63). There is a fundamental struggle for the history of education that has developed over time, raising fundamental issues about the nature of the field, where it belongs and where it is going, and its contribution to our understanding of education and the wider society. It is this continuing struggle with which this book is primarily concerned.

At stake in this struggle is the future of the field itself. Growing concerns have been expressed that the history of education faces terminal decline as a field unless it can articulate a clear vision of its role. Marc Depaepe, in his presidential address to the International Standing Conference for the History of Education (ISCHE) in Barcelona in 1992, went so far as to ask whether the history of education was worthwhile and relevant to the concerns of today: 'Does the history of education have any meaning at all? What is the relevance of the history of education to daily life, and who is still concerned with it today? And, ultimately, who will read our works?' (Depaepe 1993, p. 1). A decade later, Roy Lowe, in his presidential address to the History of

Education Society in Britain in 2002, again openly raised the question of whether the history of education was 'central' or 'peripheral', and even whether the history of education was really needed at all. Lowe was convinced that it remains central: 'Just as a society which is ignorant of its history is doomed to repeat its mistakes, so an education system which ignores its past is unlikely to achieve its own best future' (Lowe 2002, p. 503). He also observed that it was crucial to pursue a debate about what is and should be central to the history of education as a discipline:

> Historians of education risk being seen as yesterday's people in every sense of the word. . . Our best chances of long-term survival and recognition lie in an identification of what has made us and our kind significant in the past and in aspiring to sustain that challenging role into the twenty-first century.
>
> (Lowe 2002, pp. 503–04)

This book is intended as a constructive contribution to such a debate, and seeks to identify what is special and significant about the history of education in the twenty-first century world.

To understand the nature of these issues and trends, and to assess the prospects for addressing them effectively, it is necessary to consider them historically. It is true for historians, no less than for others, that to look towards the future we must see where we have come from. Part of Lowe's broader argument is that historians of education should develop a familiarity with the development of the field and to build on its past through discussion of what is now largely forgotten earlier work (Lowe 2002, p. 501). This in turn entails a discussion of what the American historian Sol Cohen described as the history of the history of education. In a major essay on this subject, published in the *Harvard Educational Review* in 1976, Cohen made the important point that such an approach should not simply be about filling in a missing chapter in the history of education as a field of study, or discussing the uses of history in schools of education, but should rather aim to 'restore the broken links between our generation and our predecessors, to fill in certain gaps in our memory' (Cohen 1976, p. 303). Examining this historiography of the ways in which the history of education has been thought about, written and presented is far from being a narrowly academic exercise. The shifting patterns of our academic labours affect status, resources, identities, careers and lives. More profoundly still, they reflect developments in the social memories of institutions, systems and societies as they change over time, and affect the ways in which these larger structures develop into the future.

I have been committed to developing historical approaches to understanding society and the world around us ever since I can remember. Throughout my academic career I have been committed to promoting the cause of the history of education, in part to deepen our understanding of history but also and no less urgently to address the nature of education, to comprehend it better and also to help to improve it. It has often been argued that there is a tension between these historical and educational objectives, but I have always found them to be not only exciting and stimulating in their own right, but mutually enriching. I am happy to subscribe to the view of the British social historian Asa Briggs that the study of the history of education is best considered as part of the wider study of the history of society, social history broadly interpreted with the politics, the economics and, it is necessary to add, the religion put in (Briggs 1972, p. 5). Yet I would insist with no less force on the educational as well as the historical value of the history of education.

William Richardson has proposed that a dichotomy has developed in the history of education between two cultures consisting of historians on the one hand and educationists on the other. On this view, the field of education, based on applied knowledge, professional concerns and current issues, has been distinct from the discipline of history, which has concerned itself solely with the academic study of the past (Richardson 1999). Such distinctions are real, and, for example, I well recall being interviewed for a senior position (in a university education department) and being asked whether I considered myself to be a 'renegade historian' – a question that was not, I thought, intended altogether kindly. Yet they should not be understood to hold rigidly and in all cases. Both 'education' and 'history' are contested and contingent categories, and more broadly the social sciences have also contributed a great deal to the study of the history of education over the years. Joan Simon, who was herself a formidable protagonist in historiographical debates (see, for example, Simon, J. 2007), acknowledged that historians and specialists in education had different interests, but argued that they could learn from each other (Simon, J. 1977, p. 71). She contended indeed that in some ways those working in education departments have an advantage over historians who are specialists in particular aspects of society or specific periods by recognizing that the educational process 'lies at the heart of the matter'. In her view, education might even be regarded as 'the core of history', on the basis that 'social achievements are stored in an external, exoteric form and must be mastered by each generation' (ibid.). Moreover, Richard Aldrich has observed that all historians of education have a duty both to history and to education, although the relative strengths of these commitments may vary according to the circumstances of audience and location (Aldrich 2003, p. 134). Harold Silver is another British historian of education who has reflected thoughtfully on the nature of the history of education, and comments that 'The history of education is in fact multiple histories, because education is itself no simple and homogeneous concept or category, and because its history can be explored in relation to almost endless variables' (Silver 1983, p. 4).

In the search for an understanding of how to reconcile education with history we can learn much from the French sociologist and professor of pedagogy Emile Durkheim, who began his famous lectures to an audience of future teachers on the formation and development of secondary education in France over a century ago. It was Durkheim who said so eloquently that it is only by carefully studying the past that we can come to anticipate the future and to understand the present, and so the history of education provides the soundest basis for the study of educational theory. History could also help us to understand the organization of education and to illuminate the educational ideals which the organization was designed to achieve, while in broader terms it helped us to understand humanity itself and the aspirations of individuals and groups. As he explained,

> only history can penetrate under the surface of the present educational system;
> only history can analyse it; only history can show us of what elements it is formed,

on what conditions each of them depends, how they are interrelated; only history, in a word, can bring us to the long chain of causes and effects of which it is the result.

(Durkheim 1956, p. 153)

It was for these reasons above all, according to Durkheim, that we should carry out historical research into the manner in which educational configurations have progressively come to cluster together, to combine and to form organic relationships (Durkheim 1977, pp. 10, 11, 15; see also Lukes 1973).

My basic argument, taking my cue from Durkheim, is that the key dynamics of the struggle for the history of education arise chiefly from its strategic location in relation to three broad areas of study: education, history and the social sciences. All of these areas themselves represent a wide and diverse range of values, approaches and interests, and each is contested and changing. Nevertheless, they each tend to express distinctive and divergent priorities in general terms. The field of education is interested in education itself, and especially with the organized provision of schools and other educational institutions for different groups of pupils and students. The discipline of history is principally concerned with the nature of changes and continuities over historical time, and itself has a strong historical connection with the broader study of the humanities, including philosophy, which are interested in the human quest for improvement. Lastly, the social sciences such as sociology, psychology and economics address a range of domains in our wider societies, and try to understand these more fully and critically in empirical and theoretical terms.

Each of these areas has a legitimate interest in the history of education. At the same time, it might be said that each embodies a different notion of what the history of education involves and of why it might be important because of its own set of priorities. From the point of view of education, the history of education needs to help to explain the problems and opportunities of education, and where possible to help to improve and develop it further. In terms of history, the potential contribution of the history of education is first and foremost to help to understand our historical past. As social science, the history of education may furnish telling examples of wider social issues. Yet there is, distinct from these separate notions of the history of education, also an inclusive vision, and a grand tradition. The history of education can seek to reach across these diverse constituencies to stake a claim in all three, education, history and the social sciences, and to build on its strengths across them. These areas of study may in other words generate a common and integrated mission for the history of education rather than divergent and competing paths or frameworks. One may acknowledge that the position of the history of education, besides being strategic in relation to these wider fields, can often be uncomfortable and insecure. For example, Donato and Lazerson, reviewing the discussions held at a special conference of historians of education in the US sponsored by the Spencer Foundation in March 2000, reflected that 'Social scientists place a high value on research design; educational historians often wonder what that means' (Donato and Lazerson 2000, p. 4). Moreover, they added,

Institutional location, disciplinary training, professional aspirations, and personal dispositions create conflicting obligations for the educational historian. As historians, we see ourselves adding to an existing body of historical knowledge. The questions we ask are rooted in the historiography of our discipline. In contrast, our connections to educational researchers and professionals lead us in another direction, to view the past in contemporary terms, finding historical questions in today's conflicts and framing the answers in terms that make sense to present-minded colleagues. In choosing one end of the spectrum, we risk neglect and rejection by the other, and are often seen as antiquarians irrelevant to the burning educational issues of our time or as 'presentists' with little appreciation of the uniqueness of the past.

(Donato and Lazerson 2000, p. 4)

For all that, the history of education has the potential to contribute to education, history and the social sciences alike, and to be equally at home with educators, historians and social scientists. Nor is this simply potential; it also has a strong track record of doing so, and of being this.

The history of education is fundamentally a form of history, and the challenges facing the field have much in common with those of its parent discipline, but its particular location and constituency have commonly presented it with specific and often more far-reaching dilemmas for the future. For example, in the late 1980s, the leading British historian David Cannadine discussed how a 'Golden Age' of writing in British history had come to an end as a result of contemporary pressures, and noted that 'At all levels of the profession, the picture is one of gloom, despondency and alarm' (Cannadine 1987, p. 180). Indeed, he warned, British history possessed 'many of the characteristics of a declining industry':

Overseas and domestic markets have been lost and are being lost to rival competitors; among those who manufacture the product, morale is low, recruitment is dwindling and innovation is failing; expenditure on research and development is inadequate and often incorrectly directed; too many goods of very high quality and great technical competence are being produced which are quite unsaleable in a mass market; and there are growing demands for government intervention to rescue this lame and languishing duck.

(Cannadine 1987, pp. 185–86)

Cannadine urged for good measure that

whether we know it or not, like it or not, or will even admit it or not, we professional historians exist to sell a product, and if we are to survive, our product must compete successfully in the market-place of consumer demand, and in the pecking order for government funding.

(Cannadine 1987, p. 190)

This all seems apt advice in relation to history in general but is especially apposite when considering the history of education. The history of education shared in these basic difficulties facing history in England in the late 1980s, but experienced even more acute problems as Conservative legislation effectively froze it out of the teacher training curriculum and history became less securely based in educational research. How should historians of education sell their 'product', and 'compete successfully', in the still less forgiving environment of the early twenty-first century?

At a more intellectual level, history in general faced a new challenge in the 1990s from postmodernist critiques of historical scholarship that posed difficult questions about established research methods and claims to knowledge. One response from leading historians was to seek a new accommodation between rival camps. Richard Evans, for example, pleaded for 'a little intellectual tolerance', while warning 'any one particular orientation against the arrogant assumption that its own methods and procedures are necessarily better than those of its rivals' (Evans 1997, p. 182). A decade on, Cannadine emphasized a similar message, as he called for historians to reduce the tendency for debate to be 'dogmatically polarised' into 'extreme and entrenched adversarial positions', to 'emancipate themselves from the spurious thralldom of dichotomized modes of thinking', and to seek to explore 'the gradations, continuums and common ground where most of the best history writing has in practice always been found' (Cannadine 2008, pp. 32–33). Similar issues arise for the history of education, itself a specialist area that has often found itself divided into rival camps and further compartmentalized into a range of interests competing for attention.

Some of the previous work that has explored these problems has emanated from North America, and especially from the US, although it is important to recognize the assessments of the field produced in many different countries around the world (for example, useful overviews by Leon 1985 for UNESCO, and Petersen 1992 in Australia). A pivotal debate took place in the US in the 1960s following the publication of Bernard Bailyn's short but influential work *Education in the Forming of American Society* (Bailyn 1960). 'Revisionist' scholarship in the field that sought to engage with broader social and cultural dimensions of education in American history was soon followed by 'radical revisionist' work that adopted Marxist perspectives rooted in social class (see e.g. Katz 1968, 1987). In the 1970s the radical revisionists began to come under criticism themselves for alleged ideological bias (for example, Ravitch 1978), and by the following decade a more pluralist 'post-revisionist' approach or rather set of approaches had begun to develop. Reese and Rury have recently highlighted key trends in this post-revisionist scholarship (Reese and Rury 2008a), arguing also that the history of education remains 'an evolving and expanding field of study' (Reese and Rury 2008b). They conclude that 'Like most other fields of research and scholarship, the history of American education is undergoing continual change and renewal' (Reese and Rury 2008c, p. 284).

Since the 1990s, debate has also concerned the implications of postmodernism for the history of education. Sol Cohen identified what he described as a new 'cultural history' of education that would cross disciplinary boundaries and engage with the 'linguistic turn' in the production of historical knowledge and understanding (Cohen 1999; see also, for example, Cohen and Depaepe 1996). Such concerns have persisted over the past decade, with Popkewitz, Franklin and Pereyra for instance emphasizing 'how ideas construct, shape, coordinate, and constitute social practices through which individuals "reason" about their participation and identity' (Popkewitz *et al.* 2001, p. x). Their methodological approaches, as they affirm, 'aim at dissolving the boundaries between what has previously been viewed as distinct – discourses and reality, text and the world – divisions that are residues of modernity', and seek to produce 'a history of the present that dissolves the textual, real, cultural/social distinctions' (ibid., p. 4).

In terms of its subject-matter, the history of education has often been defined narrowly as being about the historical development of modern systems of schooling, or a little less narrowly as concerning formal educational institutions for children and young people. Such a definition in itself encompasses many challenging issues. Yet the history of education may be taken also to be about informal processes of education and learning throughout life and society; even, as Bailyn proposed, 'the entire process by which a culture transmits itself across the generations' (Bailyn 1960, p. ix). On this broader view, the institutions of schooling developed in the nineteenth and twentieth centuries might appear to be of less significance than the many different institutions that have had an educational role in past times such as the family and the church (see also McCulloch 2005a). The nature of childhood, the family, adolescence and parenthood all have significant potential for the history of education, as key work by Aries on childhood (Aries 1960) and Stone on the family (Stone 1977; see also, for example, Pollock 1990) helped to establish. The social and historical characteristics of literacy have been much debated in relation to educational processes (see, for example, Vincent 2000; Lindmark *et al.* 2008). The history of general intellectual and technological changes is also very closely related to the history of education (see, for example, Burke 2000; Briggs and Burke 2002).

This book therefore sets out and examines a range of approaches to the study of the history of education relating to these broader fields of knowledge. With this in view, it addresses national and international debates with a range of examples drawn from relevant literature in and around the field. It tries also to develop my own understanding and professional experience of these problems in a new way. It builds on my early work produced in New Zealand over 20 years ago, when I was concerned that needs and opportunities for the field that had already been identified in the US and Europe were failing to be recognized sufficiently widely in the Antipodes (McCulloch 1986a, 1987). It was evident to me then that such issues are played out in very different ways and with distinct timings, processes and outcomes in particular national and cultural contexts around the world. It is certainly possible to identify broadly international trends and contours over the past half century, but I recognize fully that these may look very different from place to place, and that others will wish to contribute to a fuller understanding of the international field on the basis of their own experiences in other local and cultural contexts.

This book also seeks to move forward from my more recent inquiries in methodology and historiography. These too sought to build bridges between different groups. *Historical Research in Educational Settings* (McCulloch and Richardson 2000) set out to provide a broad introduction to research in the area, with a general emphasis on Anglo-American literature supported by British case studies, but also with a wider international and comparative dimension across the English-speaking world.

It reviewed historiographical controversies in the field and also methodological approaches. A later work, *Documentary Research in Education, History and the Social Sciences* (McCulloch 2004b), focused on documentary research which is closely associated with history in particular but emphasized its potential uses also for education and the social sciences. An edited collection of previously published papers in the history of education written by a range of authors in the field was intended to demonstrate the range and quality of research related to a number of key themes (McCulloch 2005a). Finally a project funded by the Economic and Social Research Council in Britain sought to adumbrate the kinds of research relating to the theme of social change in the history of education in Britain (Goodman *et al.* 2008), which then moved on to investigate the implications for social change of education in Empires, whether 'at home' or in the colonies (Goodman *et al.* 2009). All of this work was in some sense an attempt to codify the field in such a way that would provide scope for a wide range of researchers with different interests to discover connections with it and to develop it further. The current book is part of this same general project.

Much of my recent professional experience has also helped to inform my approach to this book. Over the past 15 years I have been directly involved in research assessment in the field of Education at a national level in Britain through membership of the assessment panels set up in this area by the Higher Education Funding Council and reporting in 1996, 2001 and 2008. This work helped me to understand what was being produced in the history of education, as well as in Education as a whole. It also highlighted the challenges faced by an area such as the history of education in being recognized by scholars in different specialisms.

The study is also based partly on my experience of different academic societies in the history of education around the world, as a member of national history of education societies in Britain, Australia and New Zealand, the US and also of the International Standing Conference for the History of Education (ISCHE). As president of the British History of Education Society (HES) from 2005 until 2007 I have recently been directly responsible for the further development of the field in this country. The British HES was established in 1967, and like its counterparts elsewhere has contributed greatly to promoting the field and establishing an infrastructure. In addition, over this time I have taken part in extensive editorial work, both as Editor of the journal *History of Education* (from 1996 until 2003) and also guest editor of a number of special issues of journals on different topics, and as a reviewer of many papers and books written in Britain and elsewhere. It is important to recognize the role of such work while also considering whether such societies and journals tend to isolate the field from the neighbouring constituencies of education, history and the social sciences.

How should the history of education define itself, and what vision does it have of itself in relation to education, history and the social sciences? The next chapter examines a body of literature that justified the history of education narrowly in terms of its uses for educators, teachers and policy makers in the present. This had some beneficial effects for the further development of modern education systems, but was generally unhistorical and lacked a clear base in the social sciences. Its dominant narrative was one in which the emergence and development of modern national systems of education served to promote social progress more broadly. This general approach, and the storyline that it was associated with, was widely discredited from the 1960s onwards, although it has continued to haunt and damage the field into the twenty-first century. While an international debate commenced in the early 1960s, the reaction against the traditional history of education developed at different times in different countries, as may be seen by comparing the debates that ensued in the United States and New Zealand.

Chapter 3 investigates the development of the British debate over the history of education. The field in Britain has engaged with these broader international debates, and has also often led the way in helping to develop the international field as a whole. While the traditional approach to writing the history of education was also much in evidence here, the reaction against it began in the 1930s and continued in the period immediately after the Second World War, as may be seen in the work of Fred Clarke, Olive Banks and others. Here, too, there were attempts to promote a more expansive vision of the history of education that integrated the contributions of education, history and the social sciences. In this case, the argument that underpinned this approach was that education was closely related to social change, although often in unexpected and unpredictable ways.

In Chapter 4 this is discussed further in relation to the work of Brian Simon, who sought to achieve a systematic revision of the history of education by emphasizing its political characteristics in a Marxist perspective. Simon was the most significant British historian of education of the twentieth century and indeed one of the most important in global terms. He related education to social change, but more particularly he examined it in terms of social class conflict and the struggle of the working class to achieve social equality. This approach was again based on an inclusive vision that sought to integrate education, history and the social sciences in its understanding of the history of education. Simon's work in the late 1950s and early 1960s anticipated the Marxist social class emphasis of the American radical revisionists by several years (McCulloch 2010). I would note here that after Simon's death in 2002 the Institute of Education, London established a named chair in the history of education in his honour, and I had the great good fortune and honour to be appointed to this position. I knew Simon only towards the end of his life, and I counted him as a friend as well as a greatly respected senior colleague. I regard part of the mission of the Brian Simon chair as being to recall Simon's contribution and legacy to the history of education for a later generation, but to do so in a balanced and critical manner that seeks to understand his work in its historical context. Chapter 4 is intended in this spirit.

These issues also impinge on the relationship between the history of education and educational reform. Chapter 5 examines the nature of this relationship, and the potential contribution of the history of education to a 'usable past'. This general approach to the history of education seeks to reconcile education, history and the social sciences through a critical engagement with issues of educational policy. It also considers the general failure of educational reforms in Britain and elsewhere to engage with historical issues, and the challenge involved for historians of education who seek to address contemporary reforms.

Chapter 6 discusses an emerging rapprochement between the history of education and theoretical and methodological concerns. This entails a close relationship between historical and educational aspects and broader social scientific insights. The history of education has become increasingly ready to engage with theory, a development that has enabled it to begin to address debates around postmodernism, empiricism, realism and the social relationships of knowledge. New departures in methodology, including use of a broadening range of documentary sources and the development of oral history, visual history and sensory history have also stimulated novel approaches to the history of education. In general, these indicate a healthy intellectual and conceptual quality in new scholarship in the field.

In Chapter 7, we see how these new theoretical and methodological approaches are translated into new directions in substantive areas of study. These include, for example, inquiry into patterns of social disadvantage and the exclusion and marginalization of particular groups in society, which has gone beyond the previous emphasis upon social class to address issues concerning gender, ethnicity, sexuality and disability, and a greater awareness of their intersectionality. The broad themes of teaching and learning have been reassessed with new research in the history of teachers and teaching and novel approaches to the history of learners and learning. The study of education and Empire has also responded to a growing awareness of theoretical and methodological possibilities.

Chapter 8 shifts attention from the intellectual development of the field to a consideration of its strategic challenges. In particular, it examines changes in both the internal and the external environment of the history of education. From the 1960s onwards, it has become increasingly organized as a field through specialized learned societies and journals, first mainly national in character and then becoming more internationalized. At the same time, its broader position in the teacher education curriculum and in educational research has become increasingly insecure and often untenable, to the extent that doubt has been cast on its future prospects as a field of study. From being a foundation discipline of educational studies, it has been undermined due to its supposed lack of relevance to current and practical educational concerns. It is necessary to discuss and explain the potential contributions of the history of education in this respect, drawing on its links with history and the social sciences, and helping us to raise broad questions about the nature of education itself.

I will then conclude the volume with observations on how these broad trends and debates affect the struggle for the history of education, and their likely impact in the years ahead. Is the vision of a history of education that contributes to education, history and the social sciences alike, and is equally at home with educators, historians and social scientists, attainable in current circumstances and in the foreseeable future?

2 The struggle for social progress

An older tradition of the history of education was widespread in the first half of the twentieth century that stressed the contribution made by modern national systems of education to broader social progress. This chapter examines the characteristics of this tradition of writing, and how it came to be undermined and displaced as the dominant approach to the history of education. The traditional characteristics of the history of education bore marked similarities in many nations around the world. However, the pivotal struggles over the nature of the history of education took place at different times in particular national contexts. An international debate took place over this time, but it played itself out in different ways according to specific national, social and political conditions. A powerful critique became established in the US from the 1950s onwards, leading to new work of a fundamentally different kind. By contrast, in New Zealand, for example, this did not take place until the late 1980s. The chapter focuses in particular on these two cases to consider their similarities and differences.

The educational tradition in the history of education

The orientation that was manifest in the traditional approach to the history of education was avowedly educational in nature. It reviewed the development of the modern system of public education, with the aim of demonstrating its growth and the progress that had been made in establishing modern ideals and practices. It tended to be divorced from contemporary historical debates and from social scientific theories and methods. Moreover, it became associated with outmoded and retrograde techniques, lacking historical rigour, that undermined the general reputation of the history of education as a field of study.

There were several recognizable features in this version of the history of education. First, it tended to portray the history of modern educational systems as a story of heroic progress, often from difficult and primitive beginnings and against the odds. It was often Whiggish in the sense of the 'Whig interpretation of history' as defined and criticized by the historian Herbert Butterfield in 1931: a predilection 'to praise revolutions provided they have been successful, to emphasize certain principles of progress in the past and produce a story which is the ratification if not the glorification of the present' (Butterfield 1931/1973, p. 9). This produced a characteristic teleology that celebrated the spread and growth of education, proselytized on behalf of the teaching profession, and underpinned further advances in the form of gradual, progressive reform. These were presented in turn as symptoms of gradual social and economic improvement. It was this that was often described as the liberal-progressive model of the history of education, an uncritical exercise in nostalgia and myth making written mainly by educationists for the benefit of teacher trainees.

The historical value of such work was somewhat limited, and it placed little store in social science methods and perspectives, but it fostered a convenient version of the past that teachers, educators and policy makers could use to support their own endeavours. In other words, it tended to be highly instrumentalist in nature, in the interests of contemporary institutions and policies. For this reason it tended to be regarded as unduly 'presentist', that is, concerned with the present rather than with the past, and this became a second basis for criticism of its approach. History, it was argued, should be first and foremost about understanding the past, and might be obscured and misinterpreted if concerns about the present came to intrude, so the history of education could be reproached for failing in its duty in this regard.

A third tendency, to concentrate on a list of historical 'facts' devoid of interpretation, became known as the 'Acts and facts' approach to the history of education. This trait was an unattractive and unfashionable reminder of late-nineteenth-century historical ideals. Leopold von Ranke, often seen as the father of modern historical scholarship, aimed to find out 'what actually happened' in history – *wie es eigentlich gewesen*. The key writers about the nature of history in the nineteenth century tried to formulate its character as being 'scientific', and to establish what they described as a 'science of history' (see, for example, Stern 1956a). To J.B. Bury in 1902, it meant reconstructing the past from all available sources, collecting together records from the past and 'heaping up material and arranging it, according to the best methods we know', to achieve a comprehensive but also objective and empirical study of the facts (Bury 1902/1956).

This kind of factual history has been commonly described as 'empiricist'. Gareth Stedman Jones, in one particularly influential critique, has suggested that in this form of history,

> Historical facts were analogous to the facts of natural science – discrete, atomic and supremely indifferent to the position of the observer. What the natural scientist could reveal by the use of test-tube, microscope and experimental method, the historian could uncover through the use of archaeology, philology and painstaking textual criticism.
>
> (Stedman Jones 1972, p. 97)

Stedman Jones complained that although the positivist assumptions of the nineteenth century had been decisively undermined, historians tacitly maintained this approach behind a veil of discreet silence, including a notion that the facts could be left to speak for themselves, and that developing 'theory' had to wait until enough 'facts' were collected. The history of education appeared to be one of the final strongholds of this kind of approach.

A further aspect of this kind of history of education was that it viewed development from the top down, that is, from the perspective of the leaders of the systems of public education with which they were concerned. This meant not only that it was uncritical and hagiographical about these leaders, but also that it excluded or denigrated alternative views and social groups that had received little benefit from the spread of schooling. It led to admiring biographies of politicians, policy makers and administrators of the system, and to histories of individual schools that reflected the ideals of their principals, head teachers and governing bodies. Such works, however, seemed to edit out of consideration the mistakes and disputes of such individuals and institutions. More profoundly, too, in justifying the record of the male, white and middle-class elite that dominated systems of education in different parts of the world, they left out of account issues that had faced the 'failures' of the system, girls and women, minority ethnic groups, and the disabled.

This general approach to the history of education prospered in the first half of the twentieth century, and became increasingly subject to criticism in the second half, leading often to heated debate. The issues involved become clear in tracing the historiography of education in particular countries. Examples chosen here are the US, which witnessed strong critiques of the traditional school from the 1950s and 1960s, and New Zealand, where these did not develop with any force until the 1980s.

The US

In the case of the US, the flaws of the traditional historiography were most often summed up in the work of Ellwood Patterson Cubberley, produced in the 1920s and 1930s. Cubberley's history was devoted to the rise of the common school, which was treated as a symbol of liberal progress in the modern world in general and the United States in particular. His major work *Public Education in the United States*, first published in 1919, sold over 80,000 copies by 1934, when a revised edition appeared (Cohen 1976, p. 307), and remained in use into the 1960s in textbooks in courses on the history of education across the United States. In the American context, it responded to a consensus among educators and the public in general that there was a unique relationship between the rise of the public schools and the development of American democracy. As Cremin suggests, Cubberley's work 'taught a generation of schoolmen an unflagging commitment to universal education and the institutions that further it; and as much as any single volume, it helped create an American teaching profession' (Cremin 1965, p. 42). Cohen was markedly less critical of Cubberley's work than were Cremin and others (Cohen 1976, p. 307), but it was Cubberley above all of his contemporaries who attracted the fire of succeeding generations.

Cubberley himself had offered a somewhat different explanation of what his work was intended to achieve. He argued that it provided an interpretation of American educational history in its broader historical and social contexts. According to Cubberley, indeed, it represented a new method of treatment:

> Instead of offering the usual cyclopaedic treatment of our educational development, the text furnished, for beginning students, a connected story of our

educational evolution which was closely tied up with the social, political, and industrial forces that shaped the nineteenth century.

(Cubberley 1934, p. v)

He continued:

> An effort was made to set forth the outstanding events of our educational history in graphic manner, to point out their close relation to the social, political, and national movements then taking place, and to help the teacher to see the educational problems of the twentieth century in the light of their historical development. Throughout, an effort was made to explain the connection between the history of education and the institutional efforts of the State in the matter of the training of the young; to set forth our educational history as an evolving series of events from which the recent advances in educational practice and procedure have had their origin; and to make clear the relation between our educational development and the great social and industrial changes which have given the recent marked expansion of state educational effort its meaning.
>
> (Cubberley 1934, p. v)

Since in his view the history of education, and especially the history of American educational developments, was 'too important a subject in the proper orienting of teachers to lose', he added, 'an effort was made to create a textbook that would restore the subject to its old-time popularity' (Cubberley 1934, p. v).

Cubberley's text set out to examine the development of education in America from the importation of European ideals after the sixteenth century, with an emphasis on the growth of the state system of schooling in the nineteenth and twentieth centuries. During this process, he argued, the schools had sought to address the challenges of an emerging democracy, with such effect that, as he contended,

> Within the past quarter of a century we have come to see, with a clearness of vision not approached before, that education is our Nation's greatest constructive tool, and that the many problems of national welfare which education alone can solve are far greater than the school master of two or three decades ago dreamed.
>
> (Cubberley 1934, p. viii)

It was vital, Cubberley proposed, that students of education and teachers in schools should be made aware of these developments, in order above all to reveal 'the forces which circumscribe and condition and direct and limit all our educational endeavors', and to set out 'the fundamental principles in the light of which we labor' (Cubberley 1934, p. viii).

In his Conclusion, Cubberley returned to stress the 'fundamental principles and problems' that arose from his study. The evolution of a national system of public education, he maintained, had led to general acceptance of a number of fundamental principles which represented the foundations of the modern system. It had shown that the education of all was essential to the well-being of the state, that it was the duty of all parents to educate their children, and that the State should enforce this duty by appropriate legislation (Cubberley 1934, p. 750). Moreover, the cost of providing schools as an essential state service should come from public funds based on taxation. The State should provide whatever form of education it seemed wise to add in the national interest, and this was likely to mean many further extensions of educational advantages into new directions in the future. The school provided should offer equal opportunity for all young people. The State had a right to compel children to attend school and benefit from its advantages, and should set minimum standards for all schools and expect these to be met. Public education should not be exclusive, and should allow free competition with private schools and universities. Public education was recognized as a national interest of the American people. Indeed, as he embroidered this point:

> In consequence it may now be regarded as a settled conviction of our American people that the provision of a liberal system of free non-sectarian public schools, in which equal opportunity is provided for all, even though many different types of schools may be needed, is not only an inescapable obligation of our States to their future citizens, but also that nothing which the State does for its people contributes so much to the moral uplift, to a higher civic virtue, and to increased economic returns to the State as does a generous system of free public schools.
>
> (Cubberley 1934, p. 757)

Progress had been made slowly and irregularly, and through public discussion and conflict, leading to general consensus. Teachers and pupils had been left largely to their own initiative to improve themselves, although this freedom might need to be combined with a measure of discipline imposed for the welfare of the State. Greater state control was difficult to reconcile with this established national tradition of education. All pupils should be trained for 'responsible citizenship in our democracy', and 'so filled with the spirit and ideals of our national life that they will be willing to dedicate their lives to the preservation and advance of our national welfare' (Cubberley 1934, p. 761). Education had become the great constructive tool of civilization. And finally he concluded, 'Education in a democratic government such as ours is the greatest of all undertakings for the promotion of the national welfare, and the teacher in our schools renders an inconspicuous but a highly important national service' (ibid., pp. 763–64).

In the 1950s and 1960s this general interpretation, and Cubberley himself, came under sustained attack from historians. The most powerful and widely influential critique was Bernard Bailyn's *Education in the Forming of American Society* (1960). Bailyn reacted sharply against the educational rationale of Cubberley's style of educational history. The leading characteristic of education in relation to American history, he complained, was 'its separateness as a branch of history, its detachment from the main stream of historical research, writing, and teaching' (Bailyn 1960, p. 5). It formed indeed a 'distinct tributary', leading back to a particular juncture at the end of the nineteenth century, and designed for the purpose of dignifying a new profession of educators (ibid., p. 5). It also reflected particular assumptions about the nature of history that created distortions and short-circuiting of thought. One of these, according to Bailyn, was the preoccupation with the system of public education, which failed to take account of broader familial and cultural processes across the generations. It was also important to understand the effects of education on the surrounding society, no less than the impact of society on education (ibid., p. 48). Thus the agenda for further study that Bailyn recommended was, as he pointed out, not restricted to the problems and topics bearing on schools, teachers and formal instruction, but addressed a broader set of issues in cultural history (ibid., p. 53).

Lawrence Cremin was equally dismissive, suggesting that there had been no overall rethinking of the history of education in response to broader currents in historiography since 1919. In particular, Cremin argued for a much more expansive and inclusive approach to the history of education to take account of the rise of the mass media of communications and the organization of a growing number of private, quasi-public, and public agencies committed to education but not organized as schools (Cremin 1965, p. 47). This led him in due course to produce a trilogy of books that explored the historical characteristics of education in this broader sense (Cremin 1970, 1980, 1988).

These critiques ushered in a remarkable phase of public discussion about the character of the history of education in the United States. In the spring of 1961, the *Harvard Educational Review* produced a special issue on education and American history, in which the introductory note, by Oscar Handlin, insisted that 'This hitherto neglected topic ought to form one of the central themes of American history without a command of which our understanding of our culture is incomplete' (Handlin 1961, p. 121). Sol Cohen later discerned a surge of writing after 1960 on the history of American education which he found to be 'broadly conceived, closely allied with the fields of social and intellectual history, imaginative and mature in its use of the tools and apparatus of historical scholarship' (Cohen 1973, p. 82). According to Cohen, historians of education had now 'eschewed writing about the public school as if it were unequivocally progressive and historically inevitable', and had begun to analyse institutional adaptation to social change, emphasizing the relationship of pedagogical ideas and practices to broader social, economic and political contexts, and often borrowing methods and insights from the social sciences (ibid.). John E. Talbott concurred with this view, arguing that what had previously been 'one of the last refuges of the Whig interpretation' was now to be regarded as 'a promising and hitherto neglected avenue of approach to an extremely broad range of problems' (Talbott 1971, pp. 146, 134). By the end of the 1970s, Jurgen Herbst felt able to congratulate his colleagues in the field that two decades of 'revisionism' had succeeded in transforming the history of education: 'We have incorporated educational developments into the mainstream of American historiography. . . . Their work has brought the history of education to the standing it enjoys today among our colleagues in history and education' (Herbst 1980, pp. 131–32).

This general revolt against the educational school was thus leading to an emphasis on historical scholarship and rigour, as well as on broad educational movements beyond public schooling. There was a further reaction against the liberal-progressive assumptions of writers such as Cubberley, especially evident in the work of Marxist historians who were often styled 'radical revisionists', led in the 1960s and 1970s by Michael B. Katz. According to this school of thought, modern systems of mass schooling, far from being benevolent and progressive, had developed as devices of social control that were designed to maintain existing social and economic attitudes, structures, differences and injustices. Katz in particular was concerned to dispel the 'cloud of sentiment' that seemed to surround educational reform, and to distinguish between the 'myth' and the reality: 'Popular education, according to the myth, started in a passionate blaze of humanitarian zeal; but most large urban school systems since the later nineteenth century have been cold, rigid, and somewhat sterile bureaucracies' (Katz 1968, p. 2). According to Katz, the customary 'vapor of piety' hid the real motives and interests behind the extension of popular education, which were based in 'the attempt by a coalition of the social leaders, status-anxious parents, and status-hungry educators to impose educational innovations, each for their own reasons, upon a reluctant community' (ibid., p. 218).

This Marxist approach to the history of education was reinforced during the 1970s by the writings of the political economists Samuel Bowles and Herbert Gintis, espe-cially their major work *Schooling in Capitalist America* (Bowles and Gintis 1976). Bowles and Gintis proposed a model of social reproduction in which unequal schooling reproduced the social division of labour. In this model, the historical function of mass schooling was to reproduce social inequalities from generation to generation. This strongly contradicted liberal views that held that education had sought equality of opportunity, or that educational inequalities from earlier times were being eliminated. Instead there came the uncompromising message that 'The educational system serves – through the correspondence of its social relations with those of economic life – to reproduce economic inequality and to distort personal development' (Bowles and Gintis 1976, p. 48). As Cohen and Rosenberg soon noted, 'In the place of history of education as a discipline which pieces together pictures of the schools' past, Bowles and Gintis offer a conception of ordered structural economic and social change in which education was implicated'. They added: 'The implicit notion is that history of education should not be cut off from a connection to social relations more broadly conceived' (Cohen and Rosenberg 1977, p. 114).

Nevertheless, the thoroughgoing criticisms of Katz, Bowles and Gintis were not shared by all historians of the new, 'revisionist' persuasion. Many argued that the past was neither as bleak nor as simple as the radical revisionists had depicted. David Tyack was blunt in criticizing both the 'inspirational' tradition of Cubberley and the hostility to public education evinced by Katz: 'I endorse neither the euphoric glori-fication of public education as represented in the traditional literature nor the cur-rent fashion of berating public school people and regarding the common school as a failure' (Tyack 1974, p. 9). Thus the character of the 'new' history of education was hotly disputed. The controversy between radical educational historians and others in the United States vividly reflected contemporary social and political conflicts of the 1960s and 1970s. Indeed, as in the broader 'culture wars' of the time (Shor 1986), radical revisionism emerged amid the turbulence of the late 1960s and yet appeared by the 1980s to have failed to dictate the tone of historical debate. Diane Ravitch, for example, struck a much more conservative note in her endeavour to revise the revisionists. She endorsed the earlier critiques of Bailyn and Cremin as 'liberating and fruitful', providing opportunities for 'the application of social science to historical inquiry', and facilitating the inclusion of the perspectives of social history, political history, intellectual history, urban history, religious history, and the history of science and technology (Ravitch 1978, p. 27). On the other hand, she pointed out that Marxist accounts, like the earlier liberal narratives, operated on the basis of a 'simplistic search for heroes and devils, for scapegoats and panaceas' (ibid., p. 173).

By 1987, Michael Katz could justly claim that due to the work of historians such as himself since the 1960s, 'a simple narrative of the triumph of benevolence and democracy can no longer be offered seriously by any scholar even marginally aware of recent writing in the field' (Katz 1987, p. 136). However, he was concerned with a politically based reaction to revisionism that he described as 'revisionist-bashing' (ibid., p. 137), and argued that it was now time to 'recast the debate' (ibid., p. 159). This could be achieved, according to Katz, by building on the insights of the revisionists. The task involved creating a stronger historical framework, 'one that incorporates new directions in historical writing, . . . theoretical advances, and good research'. Such work, he added, would retain a critical 'cutting edge' in the history of education, for this was 'the only kind that makes sense of the disaster that surrounds us' (ibid.).

New Zealand

A similar educational tradition in the history of education may also be identified and traced in the context of New Zealand. In this case the dominant work in the first half of the century was that of A.G. Butchers, although there were others who followed this basic approach well into the 1970s and 1980s.

A.G. Butchers' writings in the 1920s and 1930s provided a comprehensive history of education in New Zealand, at a time when little was available for students of education apart from British histories and accounts of European educational ideas. His definition of 'education' was effectively limited to the system of mass schooling that had been established over the previous 50 years, and he concentrated on the origins and rise of this system and on its teachers and administrators. His approach was intended to give the impression of objectivity, in that he claimed to provide what he called 'an independent, disinterested study of the facts carried out by the historian in a spirit of pure research' (Butchers 1930, p. ix). Butchers was an Australian by birth, and had chosen to study education in New Zealand 'in an absolutely impartial spirit of pure historical enquiry' (Butchers 1929, p. vii). This endeavour led in practise to a chronological catalogue of facts related to education. There is little that could be classed as critical analysis of the social and political significance of modern schooling in Butchers' work.

Underlying Butchers' writings were a series of unexamined assumptions about the nature and effects of education. To some extent these assumptions are benignly liberal. New Zealand's educational history is portrayed as 'inseparably interwoven with the romantic general history of the country' (Butchers 1929, p. vii). Education is treated as a symbol of civilization and progress, indeed of victory over adversity, ignorance and prejudice in the building of a united nation. New Zealand's shift from provincial educational systems to centralized organization in the 1870s is also regarded as a triumph of national progress, with the various systems 'all converging at last to the inevitable realization of the need for a genuinely national system for the whole country' (ibid.). In general, Butchers presents the evolution of a system of national, free, secular and compulsory education as socially progressive, benevolent and wise:

> The feet of the children are now definitely set upon the pathway of true national education, founded upon a scientific realization of the country's essential depen-dence upon its agricultural industries, and organised upon a statesmanlike recog-nition of its advantages of national and local control within appropriate spheres.
>
> (Butchers 1930, p. 586)

There is more than a touch of complacency in this view. Vested interests and political motives find no place in Butchers' version of educational growth. For example, he suggests that in view of the economic depression of the 1880s, 'It is to the everlasting credit of the New Zealand Government and people that throughout all this distress-ing period the development of the newly established free, public education system was continued unflinchingly' (Butchers 1930, p. 17).

In the same spirit, Butchers usually shows teachers and administrators in the best possible light, as generous, humane and visionary. He sees the rise of the teaching profession as further evidence of liberal progress, noting that 'Over the last fifty years a more rapid evolution than in any preceding period has transformed the teacher's craft in every enlightened country' (Butchers 1930, p. 6). In particular, George Hog-ben, Inspector-General of Schools from 1899 until 1914, emerges from Butchers' work as a hero and statesman of education, 'a man of farseeing vision, strong will, and indomitable perseverance' (ibid., p. 5). Butchers portrays Hogben as the embodiment of social progress as he set the agenda for the further development of the education system:

> With the appointment of Mr Hogben a new era commenced. Schooling at last became education, as we know it to-day. And education reached out beyond the old three R's to embrace manual and technical training, nature study and sci-ence; it enlarged its field of vision beyond the years of childhood and took into view the years of adolescence and young manhood and womanhood. It set about training its teachers, and sought to give both to them and to the pupils freedom to be human, and to develop as human beings can and should. And all this it did with lavish hand, free, gratis, and for nothing, to all who could and would take advantage of its generous benevolence.
>
> (Butchers 1930, p. 151)

While Rankean in his claims to be producing an impartial and scientific history, Butchers established a Whig interpretation of the history of education in New Zealand that was to become the received wisdom in the field.

Within this general framework, the experiences of different groups in society, and particularly of those who did not share Butchers' satisfaction with the 'generous benevolence' of the education system, go largely unrecorded. This is especially evident in his treatment of the education of the indigenous Maori people as yet another example of how education can secure agreement and progress. According to Butchers, after 1880, when the new Department of Education assumed responsibility for the native schools which had hitherto been separate, 'as the bitterness and hatred caused by the wars decreased and the confidence of the Maoris began by degrees to be regained, the tide of civilization and progress commenced to flow for their race once more' (Butchers 1929, p. 70). This 'tide of civilisation' is equated explicitly with 'the Europeanisation of the native race' (ibid., p. 120). Butchers claims also that through education the position of the Maori has been transformed to one of 'social and political equality with its conquerors' (ibid., p. vii). Apparently it brought other advantages too, for Butchers also sees the Maori education system as 'an object-lesson to the whole world in dealing with and civilizing an aboriginal people' (Butchers 1930, p. 5). Here then Butchers' assumptions are paternalistic and imperialist rather than liberal. Maori people are seen only from above, as the objects of policy, through the eyes of *pakeha* (European) administrators. Butchers' confidence in the beneficence of New Zealand education remains unblemished. This is educational history designed to celebrate the past and vindicate the present, calculated also to inspire student teachers with the qualities of their chosen profession.

A similar outlook to that of Butchers was adopted by Ian Cumming, the leading historian of education in New Zealand after the Second World War. Cumming's centenary history of the Education Board in Auckland, New Zealand's largest city (Cumming 1959) became a highly influential source of reference, while his key work, *History of State Education in New Zealand*, written jointly with his son Alan, was published as late as 1978 (Cumming and Cumming 1978). Cumming's work was reminiscent of Butchers in several respects. Like Butchers, Cumming was mainly interested in the growth of the modern system of mass schooling in New Zealand, and so asserted a highly restricted definition of education. If Butchers' 'absolutely impartial' approach had been something of an art form, with Cumming it assumed more of the appearance of a science. Cumming was reluctant to indulge in anything that might appear interpretative, speculative or theoretical, seemingly in the belief that a compilation of all relevant 'facts' might be relied upon to speak for itself. Readers were left to ponder and to form their own conclusions on the lessons and significance of the educational past. This approach tended to result in a collection of 'facts' about education devoid of explicit interpretation, relieved only by an occasional suitably ambiguous irony. Nevertheless, it did not produce 'value free' history. Indeed, Cumming's work was pervaded by liberal-progressive assumptions about education and social progress. Much less prone to the flights of fancy that had enlivened Butchers' prose while betraying his pretensions of objectivity, Cumming's treatment of the growth of modern schooling remained unmistakably Whiggish. With regard to educational outcomes, his work portrayed the state education system as a symbol of modern civilized values. In terms of the motives of educational administrators, too, Cumming was only interested in public explanations and rationales. He reserved his criticisms for groups and individuals who were seen to have blocked or inhibited the development of state education in recognizably modern forms. Overall, according to Mark Olssen, 'What we are offered is history at its worst – quotation mongering and name-dropping, an implausible neutrality and a poor prose style' (Olssen 1987, p. 22).

One should not single out the history of education for its Whiggish tendencies without also noting that New Zealand historiography generally was prone to liberal-progressive assumptions about the development of New Zealand society. This was the case at least from the 1890s, when the Liberal politician William Pember Reeves published *The Long White Cloud*, devoted to the slow progress of New Zealanders in building on the dreams of the pioneers (Reeves 1898). This historical model continued to inform Keith Sinclair's view of New Zealand history in his highly influential *A History of New Zealand* (Sinclair 1961). Yet these tendencies were especially manifest in the history of education in New Zealand. What Bailyn observed of the traditional educational historiography in the United States could be applied with equal justice to the New Zealand scene.

One difference between the US and New Zealand, however, was that this standard liberal-progressive approach continued to hold sway in the latter country well into the 1960s and 1970s. Very little of the debate that characterized the history of education in the US was reflected in New Zealand until the 1980s, which was explained in part as being due to the study of New Zealand history in all areas as being 'still at an immature stage of development, and full of major gaps' (Arnold 1973, p. 2). Even in 1984, one leading historian of education, David McKenzie, could still comment that 'The conventional wisdom in New Zealand educational history still owes much to the ideology laid down in the pioneering works of A.G. Butchers' (McKenzie 1984, p. 1). It was not until 1987 that a set of essays in the history of education was published that could be described as revisionist in its approach (Openshaw and McKenzie 1987). Its joint editor, Roger Openshaw, openly conceded in its Introduction that the history of education in New Zealand had been 'rather later in developing a critical perspective' than had the field in some other countries including the US (Openshaw 1987, p. 1). This delay was attributed to two main factors: the isolation of New Zealand history of education, both geographically in relation to other countries and also in relation to history and the social sciences within New Zealand, and the enduring strength of New Zealand's social and political 'myth' of egalitarianism (ibid., pp. 1–2). Stimulated also by new research in social history and sociology in New Zealand itself, writing in the history of education now began to exhibit greater interest in critical enquiry.

These fresh developments were also encouraged more broadly by social, political and cultural changes affecting New Zealand as a whole. Decades of relative security and isolation were under growing threat. The economic position of the country was at risk due to Britain's entry into the European Community and a global downturn in the 1970s and 1980s. Increasing social dissent was reflected in a new emphasis on social class, feminism and Maori protest. The conservative policies of the National government, in power from 1975 until 1984 under Robert Muldoon, were replaced by the more liberal approach of David Lange's Labour government from 1984, which also introduced increasingly free-market policies that opened up the previously sheltered economy and society in general to international competition. This was the context in which new approaches to the history of education began eventually to find broader favour.

One key exponent of the new history of education was Roy Shuker. He was earlier than most in arguing for a 'revisionist perspective' to be adopted, and in particular in engaging with the insights already well developed in the United States. In a review of the Cummings' *History of State Education in New Zealand*, he described this work as a valuable reference tool and 'a useful adjunct to Butchers' standard, but now dated, history of New Zealand education' (Shuker 1980a, p. 37). Nevertheless, he was highly critical of its tendency to parade a 'catalogue of facts, names, and legislation', with 'little provided in the way of analysis to coat the chronological pill' (ibid.). Shuker himself was strongly in favour of a more explicitly theoretical approach that took its cue from the American debate. As he noted, 'The work of the revisionist historians of American education suggests possibilities for a similar reappraisal of the history of New Zealand education' (Shuker 1980b, p. 39). His particular preference, moreover, was to follow the line of the Marxist 'radical revisionists' in emphasizing the social class inequalities reproduced in the state system of schooling as representing the establishment of a configuration of social, political and economic interests from the late nineteenth century onwards. In stark contrast with the orthodox narrative of gradual progress towards social equality, Shuker insisted that schools had been based on a a differentiated pattern of provision and served to 'reproduce existing class (and gender, and ethnic) structures' (Shuker 1986, pp. 26–27).

Another protagonist in this emerging debate was my own younger self, newly arrived from Britain in a lecturing post at the University of Auckland towards the end of 1983 and keen to make an impression. I also urged greater engagement with overseas debates, and in 1986 published a monograph emphasizing the importance of this, with a title, *Education in the Forming of New Zealand Society*, that somewhat gauchely imitated Bailyn's seminal contribution of 1960 (McCulloch 1986a). In the same year I submitted an article to New Zealand's premier journal of educational studies that analysed the development of secondary school zoning policy in Auckland since 1945, and emphasized the need for historians of education to engage in critical social and political analysis. This article concluded: 'So far as Auckland is concerned, at least, we can already point to evidence of conflict, social inequality and the maintenance of entrenched interests inconsistent with earlier reports of consensus, equality and progress' (McCulloch 1986b, p. 109). A measure of the controversy that surrounded such views at that time is that one of the referees chosen to review the article for the journal was W.L. Renwick, the Director-General of Education in New Zealand. Renwick produced a report of over 10 pages to argue that the article should not be published in the journal, in the main because of its criticisms of his predecessor, Dr C.E. Beeby. It concluded by claiming that 'the author has not developed a research design that would enable him/her to explore the big conceptual questions he/she says at the beginning of the paper he/she is interested to explore' (Renwick 1986, p. 10). I have this report still. It was disconcerting that the Director-General of Education had gone to a great deal of trouble to demolish my work. Fortunately, the joint editor of the journal, David McKenzie of the University of Otago, very knowledgeable and experienced in the history of education, telephoned me personally to discuss

Renwick's concerns and dispel my anxieties. The article was published in the journal with only minor revisions.

Such were the sensitivities that had suddenly beset the history of education in New Zealand. It was clearly necessary to pursue a critical approach, if only to raise questions about the prevailing myths such as those represented by Renwick and indeed by Beeby and others before him. However, unlike Shuker, I took the view that it would be appropriate to encourage an awareness of a broad range of revisionist ideas rather than simply the Marxist line of argument, and I also stressed that due recognition should be made of the specific nature of New Zealand's own social and historical development. These issues surfaced after the publication of Shuker's key work in the field, *The One Best System?* (Shuker 1987), which itself consciously echoed the title of an earlier contribution by the American historian David Tyack (Tyack 1974). Shuker's argument was that New Zealand's schools, instead of promoting equality as had always been claimed, had instead served to reproduce existing social and economic divisions within society. This had been a 'contested process' (Shuker 1987, p. 7) based mainly on social class, although with gender, 'race', location, age and religion as cross-cutting factors. Overall, according to Shuker, 'The result is a complex interweaving of factors, schools becoming sites of struggle as the dominant hegemony is constantly challenged and reconstituted' (ibid., p. 286).

Thus, two decades after Michael Katz's radical revisionism had been developed in the US, and at a time when Katz's approach was under increasing attack in its own homeland, a systematic Marxist analysis of the history of education was eventually produced in New Zealand. This was a significant achievement, and a further indication that the history of education was itself becoming a site of struggle. The debate that it engendered was also not confined to the national stage, for the new editor of the key American journal *History of Education Quarterly*, William J. Reese, noticed the commotion from afar and organized a review forum on Shuker's book. Invited to take part in this forum were Neil Daglish, a well established historian of education based at Wellington, Pavla Miller, a sociological historian based in Melbourne, Australia, and myself, with Shuker to respond to the issues raised (Daglish *et al.* 1989).

My own commentary was particularly critical of Shuker's work, while acknowledging its significance. I took the opportunity to point out to North American readers that while 'revisionist-bashing' had become the norm in the US and the debate was being recast, revisionism itself was only in its early stages in New Zealand. Shuker's spiritual home, I suggested rather uncharitably, was America in the early 1970s, but so far as New Zealand was concerned he was 'leading with his chin' (Daglish *et al.* 1989, p. 265). I argued that Shuker's work failed to identify the bases of 'resistance' and 'negotiation' around the character of state schooling, with the result that it did not portray the 'contested process' that it claimed to have shown. There was little trace of real barricades or blood on the carpets in Shuker's account, and a lack of clear alternatives to put in the place of the myths that were being exposed: 'The illusions of the past are exposed but we are left with little to put in their place, no rationale for amending our methods or for defending or abandoning particular practices, no strategy for fundamental change' (ibid., p. 267). I observed that the history of education in New

Zealand was becoming 'more of a contested arena, into which previously neglected groups, agencies, and dimensions are being drawn' (ibid.). Nonetheless,

> An education system shorn of its liberal apologies and weakened by radical criticisms is vulnerable to attack. We have already seen a conservative backlash in the United States and Britain; threatening signals are evident in New Zealand also. It will be the saddest of ironies if Shuker's bashing adds weight to a counter-attack from the right.
>
> (Daglish *et al.* 1989, p. 268)

Thus, I concluded, revisionism in New Zealand needed to develop quickly, and to learn to 'recast the debate' almost as soon as it had been begun, not only in order to contribute fully to an understanding of educational change in the past, but also to take part in the reconstruction of the education system in the future (Daglish *et al.* 1989, p. 268).

At the same time, it remained necessary to respond to histories of a more traditional kind which continued to be produced. One such was by C.L. Bailey, who published what promised to be the first volume of a documentary history of New Zealand education in 1989 (Bailey 1989). This work covered what it described as the 'imperial background to New Zealand education' from 1400 to 1870. I was critical of the project despite its evident ambition and the scholarship that lay behind it, because of its limited scope and the assumptions and biases involved in the selection of the historical documents. The collection as a whole was dominated by the views, plans, promises and rationalizations of a male, white, middle-class elite. It also upheld a Whig perspective of progress in educational reform and the history of education, and generally in my view tended 'to bolster and reinforce what had hitherto appeared to be a defeated and played out tradition in educational history' (McCulloch 1990, p. 121). Clearly this was a more resilient form of history than I had anticipated, and was still a potent force.

In the 1990s, a new generation of historians of education found fresh insights that were based in political and social criticism, but also recognized complexity and nuance. One major text, for example, analysed the political debates that had pervaded schooling in New Zealand throughout its history in a way that incorporated theoretical concepts while utilizing 'a genuinely historical approach to the writing of education history' (Openshaw *et al.* 1993, p. 9). The debate engendered in the late 1980s had a long term influence on the field as the dominance of Butchers and Cumming receded into the past and a broad range of critical insights came to the fore, and I was pleased to celebrate this trend in print (McCulloch 1994b). Yet the underlying resilience of more traditional approaches remained strong, and they did not disappear despite the efforts of a more critical school of thought.

Conclusions

Many other examples of a basic shift in the writing of national histories of education could be found elsewhere. A general movement away from a traditional liberal-progressive approach to the history of education towards 'revisionist' approaches has been very common, but the debate has varied in its timing and also in its specific outcomes based on the particular educational, social and political characteristics of different nations. A struggle to undermine and replace traditional national histories of an 'educational' and liberal kind has developed into a struggle to define the particular characteristics of the national histories involved. In Canada, for instance, the trend towards revisionist history developed in the 1970s and moved on towards an emphasis on 'family strategies' and the nature of childhood rather than issues of power and control in the public sphere (Wilson 1984). In Australia likewise, a new interest in the social history of education can be traced from the 1970s (Spaull 1981). These changes have encouraged reappraisals of how the history of education engages with education, history and the social sciences. In their early stages they might react against the previously dominant liberal assumptions and pieties by moving towards Marxist critiques, as in the US and New Zealand in their different contexts. In the longer term, they have also generated a broad range of critical historical accounts of educational and social change.

3   The struggle for social change

The historical study of the relationship between education and social change has become a key dimension in the history of education internationally. In the US, Bailyn's critique of the field (Bailyn 1960) insisted that this relationship was not simply unidirectional, from society to education, but was interactive in nature. According to Bailyn, 'education not only reflects and adjusts to society; once formed, it turns back upon it and acts upon it' (ibid., p. 48). Further to this, Bailyn regarded this relationship as essentially positive and liberatory in its effects on American society and the national character (see also McCulloch 2005b, p. 5). Lawrence Stone, also based in the US, chose the history of education as the focus for a regular research seminar held at the Shelby Cullan Davis Centre for Historical Studies at Princeton University from 1969, the contributors to which as Stone explained were 'all interested in the relationship between formal education and other social processes, rather than with the history of educational institutions as such, or with the history of changes in the curriculum and scholarship as such' (Stone 1975, p. vi). Stone's own approach to this relationship differed from that of Bailyn in being more modest and piecemeal, and although he remained centrally concerned with the nature of the interaction involved he concluded that 'no clear relationship emerges from which a general theory can be constructed' (Stone 1976, p. xi).

In Europe, too, this key dynamic underpinned a collaborative venture based in an international seminar held in 1979 at the Ruhr-University Bochum, related to a broader research project on knowledge and society in the nineteenth century. This initiative led to the publication of an edited collection on European secondary and higher education in the late nineteenth and twentieth centuries (Muller *et al.* 1987), with the aim of developing a systematic comparative interpretation of structural change over this period. Such a study, it was hoped, would comprehend underlying similarities or patterns across nations, rather than merely concentrating on descriptions of specific institutions and insular national accounts. More recent international conferences have also pursued this basic underlying theme of education and social change (for example, Majorek *et al.* 1998), and it has also been the subject of a seminar series funded by the Economic and Social Research Council in Britain and led by myself with my colleagues Joyce Goodman and William Richardson (McCulloch *et al.* 2005; Goodman *et al.* 2008).

The early development of this approach to the history of education played itself out in different ways around the world. In Britain, as in the US, it played an important part in challenging the traditional historiography which stressed the growth of social progress through the rise of national systems of education. The debate in England can be traced at least to the late 1930s and the work of Fred Clarke, then the director of the Institute of Education at the University of London. Clarke's approach to understanding education was based in sociology as well as history, and it was the linkage between these dimensions in the history of education that became a noticeable aspect of significant new work after the Second World War. This new literature was concerned to address and engage with specifically educational problems. The chief focus of this work was the extent to which education could promote social change, and it was this that challenged and began to undermine the older approaches to the history of education that had previously been dominant.

Acts and facts

The traditional historiography of education in Britain was fairly typical of the writing that developed on this topic in different countries in the first half of the twentieth century. As has been seen in the last chapter, this work tended to be quasi-scientific in its regard for 'facts', liberal-progressive in its optimistic narrative of gradual social progress, and uncritical of the contributions of administrators and teachers in the development of schooling. Gordon and Szreter (Gordon and Szreter 1989b), introducing an edited collection of writings in the history of education with particular reference to England, noted in retrospect three specific criticisms of this approach. First, it had an excessive emphasis on individual thinkers and writers, often with 'little reference to the period and the social environment in which they wrote', and failing to appreciate 'the gap between their noble and elevated schemes and the actual educational realities of the day' (Gordon and Szreter 1989a, p. 6). Second, according to Gordon and Szreter, 'there was overmuch concern with educational legislation, detailed provisions of Acts of Parliament and of the personalities involved in their promotion, rather than dealing with important questions arising out of legislation such as its timing, adequacy or ideological hue' (Gordon and Szreter 1989a, p. 6).

Third, they argued, too much emphasis was given to the study of formal educational institutions, especially elite institutions such as the universities of Oxford and Cambridge and the leading Victorian 'public' (independent) schools, with little reference made to informal processes of education.

Underlying all of these criticisms was dissatisfaction with the descriptive as opposed to analytical tone of much of this traditional writing, and a general lack of sophistication, stimulation and breadth (Gordon and Szreter 1989a, pp. 6–7). Other critics was even more trenchant; in the view of Gill Sutherland, for example, the study of the history of education had

> ... spent too long as an appendix to studies of the philosophy and psychology of education, or to descriptions of contemporary educational institutions: as a kind of intellectual I-Spy – spotting the first appearance of a great idea – or as a last-ditch explanation for the more extraordinary anomalies of some particular complex of educational institutions.

> (Sutherland 1969, p. 49)

With the benefit of hindsight, traditional writing in the history of education had also lacked critical insight into the complex relationship between education on the one hand and social change on the other. It was this that was to become a key issue in seeking alternative approaches from the 1930s onwards, and it was one that highlighted the strategic position of the history of education in relation to education, history and the social sciences.

Illustrations of the characteristic tendencies of the 'old' history of education are not difficult to find. One very early work entitled *Essays on Educational Reformers*, by R.H.Quick, was first published in 1868, and was updated in new editions in 1890 and 1902. This was a widely known example of the celebration of key thinkers in the growth of modern education, intended as a contribution to an increasingly scientific field and also asserting that the ideals of such thinkers should inspire teachers and lay the foundations for the future. It began promisingly enough: 'The history of education, much as it has been hitherto neglected, especially in England, must have a great future before it. If we ignore the Past we cannot understand the Present, or foresee the Future' (Quick 1868/1902, p. 1). In his treatment of this theme, Quick gave special attention to the 'rediscovery of learning' in the Renaissance of the sixteenth century, before examining the educational ideas and philosophies of several educators over the following centuries. Quick was especially enthusiastic about the ideas of the English seventeenth-century philosopher John Locke, and the late eighteenth and nineteenth century Continental reformers Pestalozzi and Froebel. He argued that it was important for teachers to study the 'great thinkers on education' (ibid., p. 504), proposing also that

> By considering the great thinkers in chronological order we see that each adds to the treasure which he finds already accumulated, and thus we are arriving in education, as in most departments of human endeavour, at a *science*. In this science lies our hope for the future. Teachers must endeavour to obtain more and more knowledge of the laws to which their art has to conform itself.
>
> (Quick 1868/1902, p. 505)

Indeed, he concluded, 'the great thinkers would raise us to a higher standing-point from which we may see much that will make the right road clearer to us, and lead us to press forward in it with good heart and hope' (Quick 1868/1902, p. 526). It remained true, nevertheless, that these ideals related only in a limited way to the everyday practices and problems of the overwhelming majority of teachers and schools.

In Scotland, with early recognition of educational studies in well-established universities, chairs in the theory, history and practice of education were created in the 1870s to which S.S. Laurie was appointed at the University of Edinburgh and J.M.D. Meiklejohn at the University of St Andrews (Gordon 1980, p. x). In England, the historical study of education was not firmly introduced into universities until the early years of the twentieth century (Gordon and Szreter 1989a, p. 5). Indeed, before the 1930s, historical studies of education in England were few and far between. In 1914, Arthur Leach, himself a historian of medieval education, went so far as to comment that 'no attempt has yet been made at any history of education in England', and suggested at this time of anti-German fervour that 'English writers, so far as they have dealt with the subject at all, have done their best to support the cult of German culture, and have ignored alike their own educational history and educational institutions' (Leach 1917, p. 2). Those that were produced failed to engage critically with social inequalities and differences. At their worst, indeed, they had combined an impregnable complacency about the virtues of the emerging education system with blindness to its defects. Some works, such as Graham Balfour's study of the education systems of Great Britain and Ireland at the beginning of the century, set out to do no more than create what Balfour himself described as an 'impartial and even tedious catalogue of existing agencies', dealing only with the 'dry bones' (Balfour 1903, pp. v–vi). Others, especially in the interwar period, identified some major social issues such as the historic tensions between the State and the Church, but remained largely indifferent to socio-economic inequalities.

One key figure in the history of education in England at this time was John Adamson, professor of the history of education at King's College London from 1903 until 1924. Adamson produced textbooks of the history of national education that typified the field. *A Short History of Education* (Adamson 1919) presented a detailed overview of the development of education in England from the Middle Ages to the end of the nineteenth century. He recognized that his scope was limited to schools and formal educational institutions, but defended this by noting 'that these institutions exist and that they have a history' (ibid., p. v). He also acknowledged that he was concerned with developments at a national level. Since there were so many differences between national systems around the world, he argued, 'the history of education is best narrated under national forms, an arrangement which is also convenient for study and indispensable for research' (ibid.). However, he also attempted to relate the history of education in England to the broad trends of western education based on Greek philosophy, the Roman Empire and the Christian Church. His work set out to trace the origins of modern public education to the early days of Christianity, and culminated with what he regarded as the founding of a national system of education in the years following the Elementary Education Act of 1870.

A later book produced by Adamson concentrated in more detail on the nineteenth-century background of education in England (Adamson 1930). Again this focused on the emergence of a national system of education during the nineteenth century. This development, involving a key shift from religious purposes and direction to the control of the State, amounted in Adamson's view to a 'revolutionary change in the national life' (ibid., p. vii), based on the ideas and principles of the eighteenth-century Enlightenment and the French Revolution. There was within this approach a notion of a relationship between educational developments and social change, but this was restricted in its scope and based on a general storyline of gradual social progress. Its culmination was the 'great achievement' of the Education Act of 1902, which established a 'State system of education' in the form of local education authorities coordinated by a national Board of Education (ibid., p. 471). Within this enlightened structure, Adamson concluded, teachers were enabled to become more fully professional and scientific in their outlook.

Adamson's underlying theme of gradual social progress was taken up and promoted further in the work of G.A.N. Lowndes, himself a local educational official in

England. This set out to demonstrate the changes brought about through the development of public education in the early decades of the twentieth century, which it described in ringing tones as a 'silent social revolution' (Lowndes 1937/1969). The building of a system of public education over this time, he argued, made possible the expansion of secondary education beyond a tiny elite group, the emancipation of elementary education from the strict regulations of the nineteenth century, the spread of technical and further education, and the emergence of special services such as medical inspection, special schools for the hearing impaired and visually challenged, and the provision of school meals. According to Lowndes, the people of England and Wales were 'transformed' during this period into 'a school-taught and substantially literate people' (Lowndes 1937/1969, p. 180), and made clear progress towards becoming an 'educated democracy' (ibid., p. 185). As a direct outcome, he claimed, society as a whole was 'continuously moving, like a biological species, from the unspecialized and undifferentiated to the specialized and differentiated', while the expansion of public education also formed 'a principal foundation for innumerable new forms of cultural, scientific, and physical activity' (ibid., p. 183).

This history of education literature tended to focus on England and, occasionally, Wales, rather than Britain as a whole including Scotland. The writings on the history of Scottish education, which developed separately, were if anything even more uncritical and devoted to charting a story of national progress. Scotland had long celebrated a distinctive national tradition dating from John Knox's *First Book of Discipline* (1560) and the early development of its major universities in the fifteenth century, through the flourishing of the Scottish Enlightenment in the eighteenth century to its system of local parish schools in the nineteenth. Histories of education in Scotland claimed to be written in an impartial and detached spirit, but nevertheless depicted the national past as a story of progress towards a national ideal of democracy and equality of opportunity. As Robert Anderson has remarked,

> When the history of Scottish education was written in the twentieth century, the *First Book of Discipline* came to be seen as a kind of expression of the Scottish *Volksgeist*, an idea which contained in itself every conceivable democratic development and which unfolded over the centuries in Hegelian fashion.
>
> (Anderson 1983, p. 23–24)

At the same time, according to Humes and Paterson, the standard histories of Scottish education were 'directly in the "Acts and facts" tradition of assuming that events speak for themselves', and therefore 'present no intellectual challenge' (Humes and Paterson 1983, p. 3).

Thus, writings on the history of education in Britain in the early decades of the twentieth century were generally of the national textbook variety, Their conception of the relationship between education and social change was limited to a celebration of a 'silent social revolution' engendered by a national system of formal education, and showed scant regard for broader historical and social scientific developments in related fields. They formed a dominant tradition in the field that was to endure well into the 1950s and 1960s. Yet even in the early twentieth century some challenge to this kind of approach was evident, and by the 1930s there was evidence of a struggle for the future of the field.

Education and social change

There were signs of alternative approaches to the history of education being attempted earlier in the twentieth century. At the University of Manchester, for example, Michael Sadler was appointed in 1903 to the first chair of the history and administration of education in England. Sadler established a history of education course that emphasized the social and comparative contexts of English education, although he never achieved an ambition to produce an authoritative work on the history of education in England (Higginson 1980). The economic historian R.H. Tawney declared portentously in 1914. when considering the progress made by the Workers' Educational Association, that 'educational problems cannot be considered in isolation from the aspirations of the great bodies of men and women for whose sake alone it is that educational problems are worth considering at all' (Tawney 1914/1964, p. 74). Yet these were relatively isolated and sporadic contributions rather than a substantial initiative.

It was during the 1930s that a significant and sustained attempt to develop an alternative approach to the history of education began to be developed, and this was associated with the Institute of Education at the University of London. The director of the Institute from 1936 until 1945, Fred Clarke (Sir Fred from 1943), was trained as both a sociologist and a historian. Clarke himself had humble social origins and had been educated at a Church of England elementary school before becoming a pupil-teacher and then taking a first-class honours degree in history at Oxford University Day Training College. He went on to be Professor of Education at Hartley College, Southampton, from 1906 until 1911, then at the University of Cape Town in South Africa from 1911 to 1929, and subsequently at McGill University in Montreal, Canada, from 1929 to 1936, before being appointed to the directorship at the Institute of Education (Aldrich 2002, pp. 90–91). Unlike his predecessor, Percy Nunn, and despite the position already established by King's College, London, in this area, Clarke favoured developing historical studies in education at the Institute and creating a chair specially in the history of education (Nunn 1937; Aldrich 2002, p. 123). In the event, this did not happen, and King's College London maintained its pre-eminence in the history of education which was to last throughout the post-war years under Professor A.V. Judges, and then under Professor Kenneth Charlton from 1972 until his retirement in 1983 (Aldrich 2009). Nevertheless, Clarke's leadership at the Institute encouraged closer connections to be drawn between education, history and the social sciences. In particular, he developed his own efforts to cultivate a new approach to the history of education that would involve a more critical understanding of the relationship between education and social change.

Clarke's approach was strongly influenced by Karl Mannheim, a sociologist from Hungary who was based in London after 1933 and became a leading member of the Institute's staff. In 1939, Mannheim wrote a paper entitled 'Planning for Freedom' which inspired Clarke to respond with a historical and sociological interpretation of English educational institutions and ideas. This briefly sketched out the social and historical structure of the education system in England (Clarke 1939), and he returned to this task in a more considered manner in a book published the following year entitled *Education and Social Change* (Clarke 1940a). Clarke's book set out to examine how the English educational tradition, so secure in its general features for many years, should adapt to the challenge of world war and to the changing circumstances of the future. This led him to develop

> an interpretation, conscious and deliberate, in terms of a social economic history, and then, in the light of that interpretation, to estimate the capacity of the English educational tradition to adapt itself without undue friction or shattering to the demands of a changed order.
>
> (Clarke 1940a, p. 1)

Clarke argued that this entailed trying to understand the historical determinants of English education, that is, 'the nature of the social influences by which the forms of English educational institutions have been determined and their practical objectives defined' (Clarke 1940a, p. 4). In particular, he observed, 'the mass of the English people have never yet evolved genuine schools of their own', as they had always been 'provided for them from above, in a form and with a content of studies that suited the ruling interests'. This tradition of 'schooling the many for the service and convenience of the few' continued to influence the nature of education, according to Clarke, and was not easy to throw off (ibid., p. 43). Moreover, he identified three separate, segregated education systems within the English education system, which he likened to the 'Free Front Door', the 'Side Entrance', and the 'Front Door on Conditions' – routes based on social rather than educational differences – and he concluded in magisterial fashion:

> We can hardly continue to contemplate an England where the mass of the people coming on by one educational path are to be governed for the most part by a minority advancing along a quite separate and more favoured path.
>
> (Clarke 1940a, pp. 43–44)

Clarke was especially puzzled by the lack of scholarly attention that had been given to these issues. He confessed that he was not aware of any studies of English social structure and class distinction that had set out to establish the social effects of these different educational routes (Clarke 1940a, p. 43). Over the following few years, he pursued this theme further, and singled out the importance of developing a history of English education. In a lecture to the Nottingham Education Society at the end of 1940, for example, he asserted that there was no satisfactory history of English education in the two centuries since the Industrial Revolution, 'taking account of the social, economic and intellectual changes and forces without which the story is unintelligible'. This was, Clarke averred, a 'great story and cruelly needed now', but he lamented that 'no one has told it', and he was convinced that it could be achieved successfully especially as cognate studies had already been carried out in such areas as economic history (Clarke 1940b).

In a further published study on the study of education in England, Clarke poured out his frustration at the lack of such works. He called for writings that could explore the connections between 'English education on the one hand and English social structure and institutions on the other hand'. This would include as the most urgent priority 'a book or books in which the story is set out, . . . a history of English education in its full cultural and social setting'. He acknowledged the existence of histories of particular institutions, and essays and biographies on particular reformers, topics and periods, but insisted that there was 'nothing for education as such comparable to what has been done in economic and constitutional history'. Thus, he complained, 'We have a vast "History of English Literature" but an adequate "History of English Education" is still to seek'. This was an 'extraordinary lack', and, he concluded, 'until it is made good we cannot regard ourselves as properly equipped for the tasks even of the immediate future' (Clarke 1943, pp. 12–13). Moreover, he added for good measure, it would be for this still unwritten history to show 'how it came about that English education works in two distinct sections, very unequal in size' (ibid., p. 39). Only in such a way would it be possible effectively to address 'that great fissure which still cuts right across English life and education, not preventing the sections on either side from talking to one another, but offering a most formidable barrier to real mutual understanding' (ibid., p. 45).

These issues seemed even more important as discussions continued on educational reform that Clarke argued 'illustrate very vividly both the disabilities from which we suffer and the risks we may be incurring through the lack of any adequate history of our national education' (Clarke 1944, p. 172). He insisted that to make a full contribution such a history should be presented 'in the full context of English social, cultural and economic evolution', especially since 'there can be no country in the world where educational forms and institutions, aims, attitudes and methods, are more directly the expression of forces constantly at work in the shaping of society at large'. Such a work, he added, would also be important for its ability to 'look squarely at the facts with the cool objective eye of a historian' (ibid., p. 173). This perhaps rather idealized advocacy of a social-historical perspective on educational debate reflected Clarke's continuing frustration at the failure of himself and others fully to seize the opportunity that was now apparent.

Clarke was a liberal thinker who regarded ideas of a rigid class structure as 'distracting', emphasized the value of adapting existing traditions to new times, and called for both courage and caution, 'lest hasty revolutionary impulses should lead to the destruction of much that is valuable and capable of incorporation into the new order' (Clarke 1940a, p. 48). He was also devoutly religious in his beliefs, and indeed his book *Education And Social Change* was published in a series of Christian News-Letter Books whose general purpose was designed 'to assist thought upon the relation of the Christian faith to present problems' (Clarke 1940a, General Preface). He was sensitive to the subtleties of English social differences, discreet in his criticisms of individuals, and willing to compromise in the pursuit of long-term reform – all qualities that helped him to become the first chairman of the Central Advisory Council of the new Ministry of Education, and to play a key role in the early development of the postwar education system.

In the context of the historiography of education, however, Clarke provided a markedly radical contribution in forging a key connection between education, history and sociology. This represented a robust challenge to the dominant tradition in the history of education, although the latter continued to be uppermost. He demonstrated the complex and problematic nature of the relationship between education and social change in a way that was intellectually challenging and engaging. Clarke was not able to fulfil his further ambitions to complete a full and detailed history of education on these lines, but left this opportunity for others to follow. His outline of educational and social relationships over time also highlighted the historical nature of the inequalities involved in the education system, between private and public education for example, and between different types of school. These were features that were open to further interpretation in the years after the Second World War.

Education and British society

During the war years, the growth of interest in Britain in plans for educational reform expressed by figures such as Fred Clarke paved the way for major legislation in the form of the Education Act of 1944 (McCulloch 1994a). This included provision of secondary education for all, although independent schools remained virtually unscathed and grammar schools continued to cater for an academic elite. Widespread debate ensued over the following two decades over the extent to which this educational reform had engendered social change, and this was a debate to which sociologists and historians made a strong contribution. Indeed, although the traditional approach to writing the history of education persisted during this time, the 1950s and 1960s witnessed an impressive flowering of historical studies of education in Britain that emphasized the connections between education and social change, including influential work by key figures such as A.H. Halsey, Michael Young, C.P. Snow, Eric Ashby, Olive Banks and Raymond Williams.

This was also more specifically a formative period in the development of social history as a specialized academic field in Britain, evidenced in new journals and the growth of interest in areas such as social class (Obelkevich 2000; Cannadine 2008, chapter 10). This helped to further stimulate new work in the history of education, and by the 1960s a wide range of research in this field was being published by social historians in Britain as in the US (see, for example, Briggs 1972; Webster 1976). Yet there was also a broader interest in the social and historical dimensions of education at this time, seeking to address the underlying difficulties of British education and society.

A.H. Halsey was prominent in this debate through his research on the relationship between education and social mobility, initially with detailed reference to the English grammar schools and subsequently developing an analysis of intergenerational change. His doctoral thesis, completed at the University of London in 1954, examined the importance of the grammar schools as the gateway to the universities and middle-class professions. It documented their unprecedented expansion between the Education Act of 1902 and 1939 through a case study based in south-west Hertfordshire, and proposed that the Education Act of 1944 had further increased equality of opportunity and social mobility (Halsey 1954). Halsey subsequently developed extensive further research on the impact of educational reforms on social mobility, including his major study with Heath and Ridge, *Origins and Destinations* (1980).

Another key figure in this debate was Michael Young, who was secretary of the research department in the Labour Party before taking up sociology at the London School of Economics in the 1950s (see also McCulloch 1991, chapter 5). His book *The Rise of the Meritocracy* (Young 1958) invented the term 'meritocracy' but was a thinly veiled critique of its social consequences. He achieved this through a historical discussion of the development of the formal education system since the Education Act of 1870, one that traced this history through to the 1950s but also projected it forward to an imagined future from the vantage point of the narrator in the work writing in 2034. According to this version of the history of education, there had been a fundamental conflict between supporters of selection by merit, who favoured the grammar schools, and advocates of equality, who championed the development of comprehensive schools. Grammar schools ultimately emerge victorious, and provide the basis for the principle of merit to pervade society as a whole. In practice, this produces a new social and political elite, 'a brilliant class, the five per cent of the nation who know what five per cent means' (ibid., p. 103). It also stimulates an uprising among older people passed over for promotion, less intelligent people who became social outcasts, and intelligent women who preferred 'romance' to science. Young's narrator expresses confidence that this rebellion can be overcome, but he is himself killed at Peterloo in May 2034.

If Young's work was a highly imaginative approach to the history of education, C.P. Snow's Rede lecture 'The Two Cultures and the Scientific Revolution', presented the following year, offered a historical argument in a more conventional manner. Like Young's 'meritocracy', Snow's arresting phrase the 'two cultures' soon became part of the English language. It was intended to highlight what Snow described as a 'gulf of mutual incomprehension' (Snow 1959/1964, p. 4) between literary intellectuals on the one hand and scientists on the other. He explained this as being due at least in part to the educational specialization between the arts and the sciences that was characteristic of England, and argued: 'All the lessons of our educational history suggest we are only capable of increasing specialization, not decreasing it' (ibid., p. 19). Indeed, he added, he could think of only one example 'in the whole of English educational history' where the pursuit of academic specialization had been successfully resisted, which was when the former order-of-merit had been abolished in the early twentieth century in the Mathematical Tripos at the University of Cambridge (Snow ibid., pp. 19–20). He developed this theme further through a discussion of the impact of the nineteenth century Industrial Revolution on English education and the wider culture. According to Snow, the public schools and the older universities had largely avoided addressing the scientific and technological changes that accompanied the Industrial Revolution (ibid., p. 23).

Sir Eric Ashby, at that time the President and Vice-Chancellor of Queen's University, Belfast, had already developed a similar historical argument in his book *Technology and the Academics* (Ashby 1958). Ashby suggested that in the nineteenth century 'a narrowly pragmatic attitude to science' had meant that 'scientific education tended to be regarded as more suitable for artisans and the lower middle classes than for the governing classes' (ibid., p. 31). Ashby saw technology as a potential means of integrating the 'false antithesis' that had developed between the sciences and the humanities, and was especially interested in changing attitudes within universities (ibid., p. 92; see also McCulloch 1991, chapter 6).

Thus, in the 1950s and 1960s in particular there was an intellectual climate in Britain that was especially conducive to historical discussions of the relationship between education and society. Two further works produced at this time are worthy of special attention for the combination of history, sociology and education that they both represented: Olive Banks' *Parity and Prestige in English Secondary Education* (1955) and Raymond Williams' *The Long Revolution* (1961).

Olive Banks' work *Parity and Prestige in English Secondary Education* (Banks 1955) was a major contribution to the literature on the historical development of secondary education (see also McCulloch 2008). It was based on her PhD thesis, completed at the University of London the year before Halsey's in 1953 (Banks 1953). Her book constituted a chronological treatment of the English grammar school between 1902 and 1944, although she was clear that in her view it was neither historical nor indeed educational in its key characteristics. Banks argued that her work was sociological rather than historical because it focused on the social functions of secondary education, and the sociological implications of the development of the secondary grammar school (Banks 1955, p. 12). The book in fact carried the sub-title 'A study in educational sociology', and it was included in the series of books founded by Karl Mannheim as the International Library of Sociology and Social Reconstruction. For the same reasons, she saw her domain of study as broadly social rather than as specifically educational. Her mentor was Professor David Glass of the London School of Economics, whose work was similarly framed in terms of general social problems (see, for example, Glass 1954).

Nevertheless, it did constitute an original and significant contribution to the history of secondary education in England. Banks was especially interested in explaining the persistence of the 'academic tradition' in secondary education, and identified the 'central thread' in this as 'the influence of the grammar school idea on the various forms of secondary education since 1902' (Banks 1955, p. 12). She found the strength of the grammar schools and of the academic curriculum with which they were associated as being rooted in the training that they gave for certain occupational groups. That is, in the interplay between social and educational factors, Banks identified a growing link between education and occupations as being of prime importance. It was change in the social and economic position of occupational groupings, Banks argued, that influenced the history of the grammar schools. The possession of certificates and examination success was the key to the opportunity to rise in the social and economic scale. Pressure to do so arose especially from the lower middle classes and skilled working classes such as clerks, shopkeepers, foremen and artisans. This in turn, according to Banks, explained the failure of efforts both before and since the 1944 Act to establish 'parity of esteem' between different forms of educational institutions such as grammar school, technical schools and modern schools. In Banks' estimation, 'If . . . the prestige of a school derives from the social and economic status of the occupations for which it prepares, then equality of prestige is clearly impossible between the non-selective modern schools and the selective grammar schools' (ibid., p. 252–53). The General Certificate of Education examination, like the School Certificate before it, was prized as the passport to a better job. At the same time, she argued, the strict doctrine of different types of schools with equal prestige, preached by the Spens Report on secondary education in 1938 (Board of Education 1938) and the Norwood Report on the secondary school curriculum and examinations in 1943 (ibid., 1943), 'could only succeed in a more equalitarian society' (Banks 1955, p. 245).

Banks therefore attributed the power of the academic tradition in secondary education not to 'the influence, sinister or otherwise, of teachers and administrators', but to 'the vocational qualification of the academic curriculum' (Banks 1955, p. 248). It was this that enabled the academic tradition to exert such pressure on all forms of secondary education. She concurred with the American social and economic critic Thorstein Veblen in his influential work *The Theory of the Leisure Class* (Veblen 1899/1973) that the social system was dominated by what Veblen had described as 'pecuniary emulation'. According to Veblen, the desire for wealth shaped the methods and selected the objects of expenditure for personal comfort and decent livelihood (ibid., p. 39), and was especially influential in institutions of higher learning. Banks concluded that parity of esteem in secondary education was likely to remain 'elusive' while this was the case, and so the movement towards educational equality would be 'dependent on the social movements of our time' (Banks 1955, p. 248).

In her inaugural lecture as professor of sociology at the University of Leicester in 1974, Banks developed this point further. She proposed here that equality of educational opportunity did not lead to a more egalitarian society, but that the reverse might be the case: 'That is to say, full equality of opportunity is only possible in a society which is no longer rigidly stratified' (Banks 1974, p. 15). This was because, as she argued, inequality in educational achievement arose not only from disparities in educational provision, but also from 'the whole way of life which distinguishes the main social classes in present-day society and which are rooted in their different opportunities for wealth, power, security and status' (ibid., p. 15). This meant in turn that the development of comprehensive schools would not in itself create a less divided or stratified society, and that there was a need for general social policies rather than specifically educational ones. The school was not itself an agent of social change: 'In so far as the school is still seen as an agency for reform it is now widely accepted that this can only be on a relatively modest scale' (ibid., p. 18). Indeed, she concluded, 'changes in the educational system can be expected to have only a limited effect on social inequalities and social stratification in general' (ibid., p. 19).

These arguments clearly carried major implications for sociology in general and the sociology of education in particular, reflected in her influential text *The Sociology of Education* which was published in 1968, subsequently reprinted several times, and went into a second and then a third edition in the 1970s (Banks 1968). They also stood in sharp contrast to the liberal perspective that continued to be dominant in educational historiography after the War. For example, Curtis (1948) was a textbook in the traditional style that portrayed the history of education unproblematically as a story of continual improvement and refinement led by a partnership between the education profession and the benign nation state, and promoting social harmony and increasing economic prosperity over the longer term. Banks' analysis of the history of secondary education, with its emphasis on controversy and conflict between opposing social and economic tendencies, helped to disrupt this optimistic liberal-progressive paradigm. It thereby contributed to the early development of more critical histories of education in its broader social, cultural and economic contexts.

Yet in some respects Banks' work was distinctive in its approach. She championed a close relationship between education, history and sociology, and was particularly concerned with the persistence of social inequalities and political debate around education. Her research was significant in helping to indicate the social dimensions of the determinants of secondary education, raising an important set of issues in relation to the role of the link between education and occupations. At the same time, she questioned the idea that educational legislation, policy, theory, teachers and administrators tended to thwart educational change, and also denied that educational influences were potentially significant as a means of promoting educational and social reform. It is also notable that *Parity and Prestige* was not particularly interested in the factors of social class and gender in the history of education, and indeed argued that the situation facing secondary school girls was 'in spite of certain differences, basically the same' as for boys (Banks 1955, p. 193).

The barrier between the independent schools and maintained grammar schools might also have been given greater attention in Banks's elucidation of parity and prestige in English secondary education. Banks' preoccupation with the differential status of institutions of secondary education was mainly confined to education supported by the State, rather than involving the private sector or elite 'public' boarding schools. She did acknowledge that public schools still enjoyed a dominant position in the hierarchy of schools, and included a brief discussion of their role (Banks 1955, pp. 8–9). She took the opportunity to stress that public schools would not easily be abolished so long as they continued to 'minister to the needs of a stratified society' (ibid., p. 245). Banks added that public schools were a greater threat to social unity than the tripartite system, 'if only because the barrier between the public schools and the maintained grammar school is deeper than that between the grammar and modern schools' (ibid., p. 246), but did not pursue this further.

A further contribution in a similar vein was that of Raymond Williams, one of the leading British sociologists of the postwar period who also emphasized a historical approach. Williams was a key exponent of theories of cultural change and popular culture, also expressed in Richard Hoggart's work *The Uses of Literacy* (Hoggart 1958). His book *Culture and Society, 1780–1950* (Williams 1958) was a critical history of ideas and values in Britain since the eighteenth century. *The Long Revolution* (Williams 1961) developed its key themes further, attempting in particular to define and explore the social and cultural transformation of the past two centuries. He conceived this very broadly as the combination of a democratic revolution, an industrial revolution, and a cultural revolution. The third of these, involving 'the aspiration to extend the active process of learning, with the skills of literacy and other advanced communication, to all people rather than to limited groups' (ibid., p. 11), was in Williams' view bound up with the other two, the growth of democracy and the rise of scientific industry, although it was still at an early stage even in the more advanced countries such as Britain. As a central aspect of this, he examined the historical development of a number of key cultural institutions, including the formal education system, and devoted a chapter to the history of education in its relationship with British society.

Williams' chapter on the history of education in *The Long Revolution* stands out as a fascinating contribution to the topic by a leading scholar at the height of his powers. He pointed out that both the organization and content of education were closely related to the broader culture and society. It was this 'organic relation' (Williams 1961, p. 145) that required investigation in his view: 'I propose to examine the history of English education from this particular point of view: to see the changing complex of actual relations, in social training, subjects taught, definitions of general education, in the context of a developing society' (ibid., p. 147). Moreover, he added, this would have significance for understanding current educational issues, for, as he proposed, 'since we ourselves are not at the end of history, but at a point in this complex development, the historical account will necessarily lead to an analysis of our own educational values and methods' (ibid.).

Williams' historical study of this theme took him back to early English schools in the sixth century AD, as he argued that these not only had a vocational role for intending priests and monks, but also involved a particular social training and the definition of a proper general knowledge. He traced the development of different kinds of schools and curricula following the Renaissance and Reformation of the sixteenth century and then focused on the effects of the industrial revolution in the eighteenth and nineteenth centuries, leading to a system based rigidly on social class divisions. His analysis of the curriculum that emerged in the nineteenth century suggested a compromise between public educators, industrial trainers, and traditional humanists. In the twentieth century, he argued, the inherited framework had been expanded and improved, with the public educators coming to the fore but other historical traditions remaining resilient. Indeed, according to Williams, 'The fact about our present curriculum is that it was essentially created by the nineteenth century, following some eighteenth-century models, and retaining elements of the medieval curriculum near its centre' (Williams 1961, p. 172). He concluded by contrasting this historically inherited curriculum with the kind of broad prospectus that would be necessary for the further growth of a democratic society and culture, and declared in challenging terms:

> The privileges and barriers, of an inherited kind, will in any case go down. It is only a question of whether we replace them by the free play of the market, or by a public education designed to express and create the values of an educated democracy and a common culture.
>
> (Williams 1961, p. 176)

Conclusions

The historical perspectives on the relationship between education and society addressed by Banks, Williams and others also posed a challenge to the traditional historiography of the history of education. This new work placed much less emphasis on a chronological and descriptive treatment, and much more on social, cultural and political analysis. Taking its cue from Fred Clarke, it struggled to understand the nature of the historical relationship between education and social change. Banks took the view that educational change could do little to change the nature of society, and that social change was a prerequisite for educational change; Williams proposed that education was part of a broad range of institutions that had contributed greatly to social change over the longer term. Moreover, if Williams in particular could detect a 'long revolution' since the eighteenth century in which education had especially prominent, such a conception was more complex and intellectually engaging than the complacent vision of a 'silent social revolution' championed by G.A.N. Lowndes. The insights of the social sciences, especially sociology, were being allied with historical methods and educational ends.

This new historical literature in England had emerged separately from and earlier than the revisionism associated with Bailyn and Cremin in the US, and with distinctive characteristics of its own. It took up the themes of social mobility, cultural elites and social class that were uppermost in British political debate of the period to generate questioning and radical interpretations of the history of education. Such an approach was starkly opposed to the older style of history of education that persisted and remained dominant in many textbooks and courses. It was also espoused and taken into an even more radical direction by another key intervention in the field at this time that insisted on the need not merely to pay attention to social change, but to struggle for social equality.

4 The struggle for social equality

Brian Simon (1915–2002) was by common consent the most significant historian of education produced in Britain over the past century. He published a very large corpus of work from the 1950s onwards, continuing through a rapidly changing educational, social and political context into the early twenty-first century. His key historical work, for which he is most widely known, is a four-volume history of education in Britain since 1780, of which the first volume was published in 1960 and the final one in 1991. This was one of a large number of important contributions to the field. He was an early leader of the History of Education Society in Britain from its foundation in 1967, as well as President of the new British Educational Research Association in 1977–78, and also helped to establish the International Standing Conference for the History of Education (ISCHE) in the 1970s. Probably his greatest achievement was in developing a rationale for the history of education that built further on the idea that it should be based in the relationship between education and social change that was current in Britain in the 1940s and 1950s (see also Simon's published memoir, Simon 1998; also Cunningham and Martin 2004).

Exploring the relationship between education and social change offered new opportunities as a rationale for the study of the history of education and as a basis for critical scholarship. It also provided scope for different interpretations about the nature of this relationship. In the 1950s and 1960s, Simon developed a potent line of argument within this broad outlook that took the field into a new direction in the British context, with significant implications also in other countries. Simon strongly supported the view that the history of education should be about the relationship between education and social change. As a Marxist, however, he interpreted this relationship specifically in a framework of social class conflict, with the ultimate end being social equality and the liberation of the working class. As Rattansi and Reeder have argued, Simon regarded the struggle for the history of education in activist terms, as being not simply academic in nature but also political and ideological (Rattansi and Reeder 1992). The aim was not only to discredit the traditional liberal-progressive historiography, but to encourage broad support for an argument that would actively promote the attainment of social equality for all. This chapter explores Simon's historical work in detail, with the help of his personal archive based at the Institute of Education in London, to assess his concept of the struggle for the history of education, and the broader implications of this.

Brian Simon and the history of education

Simon drew on three key sets of educational influences to inform his approach to the history of education. The first was his family and school background, which imparted a strong sense of citizenship and social justice and a commitment to oppose fascism. Second was his period as a student at Trinity College Cambridge, where he became a Marxist and joined the Communist Party in 1935. The third was his training as a teacher at the Institute of Education in London, which introduced him to the social and historical ideas of Fred Clarke.

Simon's family background was both socially privileged and politically advantaged. He was the second son of Sir Ernest and Shena Simon, who were leading members of the liberal intelligentsia devoted to educating their children in liberal values and active citizenship in preparing them for public life. Sir Ernest Simon was a successful industrialist who became Lord Mayor of Manchester and a Liberal Member of Parliament before founding the Association for Education in Citizenship in 1934 (Stocks 1963; Jones 2004), while Shena was a feminist and political activist who was appointed to be a member of the influential Consultative Committee of the Board of Education (Martin 2003). Brian was also educated at Gresham's School in Holt, Norfolk, which had a national reputation at this time under its headmaster J.R. Eccles for inculcating progressive values in the offspring of the Liberal elite (Eccles 1948; McCulloch and Woodin 2010b). His education was taken forward when he spent several months in 1933 at Salem School in Germany. Salem had acquired an international recognition for its approach to character training, but while Simon was staying there Adolf Hitler came to power in Germany and the school's headmaster, Kurt Hahn, was imprisoned. In his unpublished autobiography, much fuller and franker than the published memoir and also written in the 1990s, Simon recalled that this experience had 'encouraged a certain independence of mind after the rather suffocating and certainly highly controlled life at Gresham's' (Simon n.d. [1990s]). It also heightened his political awareness in stark fashion at a time of growing opposition to fascism among his generation.

This political understanding was consolidated at the University of Cambridge when Simon joined the Communist Party. He was open in his commitment, and active in political campaigns then and later. In retrospect, as he conceded in his unpublished autobiography, the hope or 'vision' of socialism represented in the Soviet Union 'proved an illusion', and he and his generation of left-wing fellow travellers 'blinded ourselves to the human horrors perpetrated there'. Nevertheless, he insisted that joining the CP in Cambridge in 1935 had been the only serious and honest option in resisting capitalism, fascism and war, and that the CP and its ideas provided a strong foundation for developing a radical educational programme (Simon n.d. [1990s]). He maintained his Marxist views throughout the Second World War, when he served in the British Army from 1940 until 1945, as a teacher at a number of schools of different kinds from 1945 until 1951, and then as a lecturer in education at Leicester University College from 1951 onwards. Unlike many of his generation, moreover, he remained loyal to the CP despite the Hungarian uprising against the Soviet Union in 1956 (Pelling 1958, chapter 10).

Simon's views about the history of education were also strongly influenced by his period of training to be a teacher at the Institute of Education, London, from 1937 to 1938. Here, he was deeply influenced by the ideas of Fred Clarke about the relationship between schools and society. In an essay that he wrote at the Institute of Education in 1937, he argued that the function of schools in a changing society should be to educate for adaptability and change, in order to create 'a society in which nothing is taken for granted, in which everything is questioned, analysed, and examined' (Simon 1937). In this respect, he was clearly aware of his debt to Clarke, and he was frank in his praise for Clarke's role in sketching out what in Simon's view was

> a new function for the educational historian, that of unravelling the social and historical influences which have played so potent a part in shaping both the schools and what is taught inside them; and, most important, of distinguishing the genuine educational theory from the rationalization which seeks to explain away rather than elucidate.
>
> (Simon 1966, p. 95)

According to Simon, it was precisely this that enabled the history of education to take on a new aspect, 'as a vital contribution to social history – rather than a flat record of acts and ordinances, punctuated by accounts of the theories of great educators who entertained ideas "in advance of their time"' (Simon 1966, p. 95).

Towards the end of his life, Simon remained committed to the central lesson that historical study can and should make a direct contribution to an understanding of the relationship between educational and social change, as being 'the crucial issue that confronts the historian', and continued to give full credit for this lesson to Fred Clarke (Simon 1994). He was also willing to concede that the impact of educational change upon society tended to be unpredictable and often led to unexpected outcomes (Simon 1985a). In a key essay published in 1985, 'Can education change society?', Simon observed that the changed consciousness of individuals and groups that resulted from new circumstances and forms of activity profoundly influenced social development (ibid., p. 22). In the English context, as he maintained, the national system of schooling had been established in order to reinforce existing social and economic relations, but had become itself a site of conflict. Thus, he concluded,

> Modern education systems, it seems to me, are an area where the interests and objectives of different social classes, strata and even groups meet and very often clash. . . . In this situation, as the historical record surely makes clear, there is scope for a variety of solutions; which of these will be successful depending on the balance of forces at any particular time
>
> (Simon 1985a, p. 27)

He did not therefore expect education systems with such a background 'to act directly and immediately to transform that society – say in a socialist direction' (Simon 1985a, p. 28). Comprehensive education, he added, should not be judged or evaluated by its success or otherwise in achieving such a change (ibid., p. 28). According to Simon, it was the long-term outcomes that were of greater importance, and in this sense he was confident that education could indeed change society (ibid., pp. 29–30).

Simon's interpretation of this relationship was decisively shaped by Marxist ideology with the historical class conflict at its heart. He viewed comprehensive schools, designed for all abilities and aptitudes, as a key site of struggle. Unlike the so-called tripartite system of secondary education which retained an academic elite in the grammar schools and left the majority of pupils in secondary modern schools with low standing and few opportunities, the spread of comprehensive schools would, he insisted, mark 'an important victory in the constant battle against privilege' (Simon 1949a, p. 486). Marxist educational theory, in its demand for the comprehensive school, was therefore, according to Simon, a direct challenge to the theory and practice of bourgeois education, and represented a rallying point in the educational class struggle. In particular, he insisted that intelligence testing at the age of eleven – known as the 'eleven-plus' – was 'highly reactionary in content'. Indeed, he proposed, 'The demand for the comprehensive school rests fundamentally on a criticism of this practice, since it denies the possibility of dividing children according to their *future* success at the age of eleven' (Simon 1949b, p. 695).

Simon's historical perspective was closely related to his Marxist approach to current educational problems. In a Communist Party circular for the Lancashire and Cheshire district in 1946, he pointed out that although the education system often appeared part of the natural order of thing, the Marxist 'is equipped to analyse and to understand the true function of these institutions, maintained and dominated by the ruling class for their own purposes'. He insisted that this situation was readily apparent from the historical record:

> The chief lesson that history has to show with regard to education is that the ruling class has always without exception used education ... for its purposes as a buttress to support and perpetuate its dominating position, and has always opposed the extension of education to other classes except to the limited extent which, at certain periods, may have been necessary for its more effective domination.
>
> (Simon 1946)

Thus, he continued, working-class schools in the nineteenth century had been essentially 'education on the cheap for the masses', and since the Elementary Education Act of 1870 'the ruling class working through the bourgeois state has dominated the education system both as regards its *form* or structure and as regards its *content*' (Simon 1946). In this way a rigid class structure had been maintained, with only a narrow ladder of opportunity for the most academically able children from the working class. Against this historical background, he proposed, the significance of the Education Act of 1944 was that the position of the ruling class had been weakened and that of the working class strengthened due to the persistent agitation of the labour movement, which should now continue to work for further educational reforms (ibid.).

This emerging historical perspective was in stark contrast to the standard line taken by histories of education which continued to emphasize the gradual social progress associated with the spread of modern schooling. One notable example of this was a collection of papers under the title *Pioneers of English Education* based on a series of lectures presented in 1951 and edited by A.V. Judges, the professor of the history of education at King's College London (Judges 1952). Judges argued in his introduction to this work that the education system in England had benefited from the pioneering efforts of English reformers in the nineteenth century, as opposed to the Continental educators who had hitherto received most of the credit for experimental and radical approaches. Sir Philip Morris, Vice-Chancellor of the University of Bristol, helped to set the prevailing tone for Judges' collection with his study of the English tradition in education (Morris 1952). He pointed out the close relationship between the development of the education system and the character of the broader society, and suggested that education had contributed greatly to social improvement over the past century. In the chapters that followed, a number of distinguished historians and other educators (all men) explored the generally beneficent influence of the leading English (male) reformers in building up the State system of education. The set was completed by Sir John Maud, then the Permanent Secretary at the Ministry of Education, who celebrated the role played by twentieth-century administrators in developing the English tradition further. In this, he praised the efforts made to promote democracy and freedom through the steady devolution of powers to local education authorities, schools and teachers (Maud 1952).

None of this impressed one stern critic, writing anonymously but with a style and message that were surely those of Brian Simon. A trenchantly critical review of Judges' book is pasted into a scrapbook of reviews and writings in the 1950s, in Simon's personal archive which is now based at the Institute of Education, University of London. This author demanded:

> Is the history of education important? Students are given it at college and university, teachers at refresher courses. Today, more and more books are being written, courses of public lectures organised. Clearly it is considered important. But the question is: *what sort of history?*
>
> (Anon. [Simon] 1953)

The reviewer complained that Judges' volume spoke only for the middle class, whereas the working-class struggle for education had been entirely absent. Indeed, 'The real causes of educational developments are not revealed in these highly respectable lectures, which, with one or two exceptions, skate on the surface in a superficial manner, as if fearing to probe any deeper'. The review continued:

> It was, in fact, the working class, in the 50-year-long struggle *against* the bourgeoisie, who won the shorter day and so made education possible. It was the working class, in the sharp and prolonged struggles for the franchise, who made mass education inevitable. And it was the working-class leaders, men like Lovett and many others, who stated unequivocally what sort of education they wanted. These were the real pioneers of English education.
>
> (Anon. [Simon] 1953)

This meant that knowledge of the history of education was important:

> It clarifies the real issues, strengthens us in our struggle, points the way forward. But it must be *our* history, one that recognizes the part played by the working class, and which assesses the spokesmen of the bourgeoisie in the light of their real motives.
>
> (Anon. [Simon] 1953)

It concluded roundly that this working-class struggle continued to the present day, with the purpose of 'freeing our children from exploitation in the factories at the age of fifteen, and so making possible a real secondary education common to all' (Anon. [Simon] 1953).

This reviewer was surely Simon himself, but it was certainly on this basis that Simon set out to produce an alternative version of the history of education, concerned with the social class struggle for social equality. He did so at the same time that he was achieving prominence and a high national position in the British Communist Party in the late 1950s and early 1960s, and his commitment to history was closely related to his political activism. It represented an approach to history that Raphael Samuel was to describe as 'people's history', broadening the basis of history, enlarging its subject matter, making use of new materials and offering new maps of knowledge. According to Samuel, such work tended to be oppositional and offered an alternative to orthodox scholarship. It was also 'shaped in the crucible of politics, and penetrated by the influence of ideology on all sides' (Samuel 1981, p. xx). Simon's history was a significant example of this (see also McCulloch 2010).

Studies in the history of education

Of his many works, Simon's massive four-volume history of education is surely his outstanding and defining contribution. What became the first volume in the set covered the period from 1780 to 1870, and explored the nature of educational reform in England during the Industrial Revolution, up to and including the Elementary Education Act of 1870. The second volume took the story up to 1920, the third covered the interwar period, and the fourth and final volume surveyed half a century of educational change from 1940 to 1990. Even if the ensemble as a whole was modestly entitled 'Studies in the History of Education', it has come to be regarded as the standard text for the history of education in England, a position it retains today, over half a century after the publication of the first volume.

This key work was written over a 30-year period that was marked by massive upheavals but also profound continuities. The first volume (Simon 1960a) was published in 1960, in the heyday of Harold Macmillan, a Conservative prime minister whose party had just won three consecutive general election victories. This was at a time when the Ministry of Education resisted active intervention in curricular issues. It was at the height of the Cold War and the space race between the United States and the Soviet Union. The second came out in 1965 (Simon 1965), during Harold Wilson's first Labour government, at the time of Circular 10/65 and the spread of the comprehensive schools. The third, in 1974 (Simon 1974), emerged at a time of increasing economic and industrial tension, with the fall of Edward Heath's Conservative government, and shortly before the launch of the so-called 'Great Debate' in education. The fourth volume (Simon 1991) was published in 1991, soon after the downfall of Margaret Thatcher who herself had presided over three consecutive Conservative general election victories, in the aftermath of the Education Reform Act of 1988 which among other things introduced a legally enforced National Curriculum. It was also after the fall of the Soviet Union and the rise of a new world order, not after all the end of history but the beginnings of a new and perhaps even more threatening phase of human development.

In this history, Simon focused his attention squarely on the social significance of the differing educational routes that had developed in England. He was clear as to how this version of history differed from most accounts: 'No doubt there was, in one sense, a "silent social revolution" at this time, but the changes brought about in the educational system were ultimately the outcome of battles fought out amid much noise and dust'. Thus, he insisted,

> This is not merely a story of philanthropy and growing enlightenment, resulting in a continuous upward curve of development but rather a history of break-throughs and retreats from which the lesson to emerge for the Labour movement was that nothing is gained (or retained) without persistent and determined pressure.
>
> (Simon 1965, p. 363)

Moreover, as he acknowledged, 'Even this may fail to avert severe setbacks' (Simon 1965, p. 363). In this way, Simon's work asserted the importance of social class conflict and social inequalities in understanding the history of education.

It was Simon's own political beliefs that underlay his specific interpretation of the history of education. This was essentially the story of what Simon called 'the working-class struggle for education' (Simon 1960a, p. 14). According to Simon, at least since 1832, 'It is primarily in the working-class movement that there is expressed the fervent belief in the power of human reason, in science, in education as an essential means to individual and social development' (ibid., p. 365). This in turn was part of what Simon regarded as 'the continuing struggle for socialism – for a society in which classes would be abolished and the opportunity for full human development made equally available for all' (ibid., p. 367). In Simon's version of the history of education, the originators of the state education system in the nineteenth century such as Robert Lowe and Kay-Shuttleworth spoke for middle-class interests in undermining those of the organized working class, in education as in society as a whole. It is the contest between these opposing class interests that Simon portrays as playing itself out in the domain of education throughout the nineteenth and twentieth centuries.

In the first volume, Simon explored the diverging interests of the middle class and working class in relation to education in the nineteenth century, and the emergence of a struggle between them (Simon 1960a). Over the previous years, Simon had rehearsed this overall argument in his own private notes. In his view, after the middle class gained economic and political power in the middle decades of the century, the Elementary Education Act of 1870 represented the consolidation of a class-based system of schooling in which the working class was largely confined to elementary schools (Simon 1955a). At the same time, he argued, the industrial working class also began to emerge as an independent political force with its own aims for education:

> In line with these political and economic demands, this class also demanded the right to a full education, which they saw as the means to political emancipation. The more class conscious sections, therefore, consciously rejected the ideology (i.e. political economy) and the educational ideas of the bourgeoisie, and evolved their own educational theory and practice in opposition to that of the bourgeoisie.
>
> (Simon 1955b)

Nevertheless, Simon concluded, the bourgeoisie, 'now holding the reins of power, utilises for the first time the direct apparatus of the state apparatus, and sets out deliberately to construct an educational system which will buttress and develop its power' (Simon 1955b).

As he noted privately on the eve of its publication, the book was a systematic attempt 'to interpret education in the nineteenth century in terms of classes – class relation and class struggle'. It was, as he also noted, one of the first books to have done this, and he felt that 'the thesis has been (reluctantly) accepted' (Simon 1960b). By Simon's own estimation, he had shifted the history of education from being 'a record of benevolently inclined individuals' to 'a descriptive analysis of the contemporary political (class) significance of educational ideas and change', so that, as he maintained,

> . . . integrally connected with economic, technical, social, religious and political developments generally the field of education is seen in this sense as an area of class struggle – wherein is reflected wider economic and political struggle of classes. It is only in relation to the wider struggle that the educational struggle and educational change take on meaning or can be fully understood.
>
> (Simon 1960b)

This was an entirely different view of the history of education than had been offered by A.V. Judges and his distinguished colleagues only a few years earlier.

Simon made a key distinction in his work between institutional forms and the content of activities, although he saw them as forming a unity and proposed that they should be dealt with together. He argued that form and content were both influenced and changed as a result of external and internal influences that operated in a complex manner. In order to isolate these influences for analysis, and to decide which were most important, it was necessary to formulate a philosophical interpretation of social development. Hence, he reasoned, it was important 'to analyse the underlying causes of social change, their effect on class relations, establish the relation of superstructure to substructure, and show in turn the relation between ideological changes in education' (Simon 1960c). However, this should not be seen as a mechanical process: 'Since education has a material existence it acts itself on the superstructure. The process of cause and effect is dialectical, and interpenetrative'. Overall, form and content could only be understood when studied historically in its development, and in its social relations. In his view, external influences that affected schools in general were changes in the mode of production, changes in class relations resulting from this, and changes in ideology due to both of these. Such ideological changes were the 'immediate motive force' for education (ibid.).

Simon had initially intended his volume to include historical developments up to the end of the nineteenth century, and to emphasize the relevance of the history for addressing the contemporary situation, but the account that was published in 1960 was perhaps all the more effective for being more restricted and relatively restrained. In planning a second volume, his preliminary plan was to cover an extended period from 1870 to 1940, although eventually it concluded in 1920. He envisaged the book as exploring a new phase in the struggle for education, with the challenge of the working class at a higher level and more conscious than before due to the rise of socialism in the mid-1880s:

> This is the challenge. The working-class movement was becoming increasingly clear as to what they wanted and how they would get it (socialist theory). Whereas previously the working class had made a largely unconscious challenge to the ruling class, now it was a conscious challenge, with clear objectives, backed by political and economic understanding (but deal here with the different groupings among the workers – the Reformists, the largely neutral and the Marxist).
>
> (Simon 1961)

As he envisaged the argument, in the late nineteenth century the bourgeoisie attempted to prevent the development of a socialist consciousness and political action among the workers, but the working class resisted by fighting for free education, secular education and elected school boards and against child labour. Then there would be a chapter on the Education Act of 1902, which he saw as 'crucial', since 'all the contradictions and struggles around education come to a head in the fight around this Act'. The fight for secondary and higher education in the early decades of the twentieth century would follow, leading on to the 'Labour compromise' following the First World War which would show the 'semi-revolutionary upsurges' of the period and also 'the way the distortion of the policy "secondary education for all" was brought about, thus partially disarming the labour movement in the between wars period'. Taking the study through to include the Education Act of 1944 would, he thought, 'indicate the character of the continuing struggle after its passage to show that the 1944 Act did not, as is so often claimed, alter the class basis of education, although, still unimplemented, it comprised much that was progressive' (Simon 1961). Here again the activist instinct is evident in how Simon approached his history.

On the basis of Simon's first two volumes his reputation as the leading historian of education in Britain was now secure. His plan for the third volume was similarly ambitious in that it anticipated completing the work from 1920 up to the present day. In the event, it restricted itself to a detailed study of the 1920s and 1930s. This volume emphasized the notion of 'social control' which was a widely used term in Marxist sociology and history of education in the late 1960s and 1970s (e.g. Johnson 1970; Sharp and Green 1975). In his background notes rehearsing the argument, he highlighted the 'crystallised structure' of the education system in the 1930s:

> The system, then was a total system of social control – related very closely to occupational structure; each section of the system served specific social/occupational ends – i.e. the system "reflected" and "fed" the occupational/economic structure as it existed at this time.
>
> (Simon 1971)

The book included a critical examination of the social class inequalities of secondary education in the early decades of the twentieth century. According to Simon,

> Since the outset of the century the central question in the field of public education has been the nature and scope of the secondary school system, the curriculum and means of access, the implications in terms of organization and finance, the respective share in shaping developments of central and local authorities.
>
> (Simon 1974, p. 10)

He depicted an underlying conflict between, on the one hand, pressures to extend school life and to improve the quality of education for the majority of the age range and, on the other, a determination to maintain the separate and limited system of elementary education that had been established in the Elementary Education Act of 1870 (Simon 1974, p. 10). In the 1920s and 1930s in particular, he argued, an official emphasis on economy had matched an elitist ideology 'to programme secondary education only for an elite with, for the majority, merely ancillary provision to promote togetherness in the tasks of making capitalist industry and social relations work' (Simon 1974, p. 318).

By the time that Simon came to complete his work with a fourth volume, he had retired from his academic position at Leicester University and had also distanced himself from the Communist Party. Nevertheless, he remained politically active and took a leading part in opposing the Education Reform Act of Margaret Thatcher's Conservative government in the late 1980s. The fourth volume might be considered a fairly orthodox political narrative of the period from 1940 until 1990, yet it provided an opportunity to assess in detail the spread of comprehensive education and the educational struggles of his own generation. He continued to view this history in terms of social class struggle, as he stressed in his background notes: 'Analysis must show changing relations between educational opportunities (levels) and class / occupational structure – so relating educational change specifically to social change' (Simon 1990). He tried to relate these changes to theoretical issues raised by Pierre Bourdieu and the Italian Marxist Antonio Gramsci, whose ideas had become popular in the 1970s and 1980s, although he found it difficult to accommodate this new thinking:

It should also (following Gramsci!) look at the whole initiative by the govern-ing class to retain hegemony (!) through not only the education system, but also through adult education and similar institutions (press, TV, etc.); the fight-back (insofar as there was one) against all this.

(Simon 1990)

In his plans for the fourth volume, Simon continued to seek to emphasize points of social and political conflict in relation to education. His approach to the educational policies of the Conservative government in the 1950s focused on the problematic and contentious as being of particular interest, for example, as he noted in the diary that he maintained on his research for this volume,

The contradictions emerging (or sharpening) during this period between the needs of the economy for higher levels of skills/knowledge (to enhance produc-tivity and therefore maintains Britain's place versus competitors) and an inert and *increasingly* crystallised educational structure (C.P. Snow used the term "Two Cultures" in 1959).

(Simon 1985b)

He was torn between his political activities, which consumed much of his time as the Conservatives' educational plans progressed, and the completion of this project. In May 1988, he noted that he had spent several days clarifying the outline of the book 'after all the frenetic activity on the Baker Bill'. This was now 'calming down', with the Education Bill now in the House of Lords and the key debate on the curriculum currently being held. 'I've done all I can', as he reflected, and he resolved from then on to turn again to his history (Simon 1988).

In Simon's history, the 1960s marked a high water mark in the working-class strug-gle for education, especially through the spread of the comprehensive schools and new developments in primary education and the universities. A Labour government was responsible for much of these educational policies between 1964 until 1970, but Simon was not willing to give full credit to the government's endeavours: 'This must not be presented as a success story; it should be a cool, dispassionate assessment of the position' (Simon 1977). One reason for this was that he was convinced for many years that Circular 10/65, which provided the basis for local education authorities to reorganize secondary education on comprehensive lines, should have made it com-pulsory for all secondary schools to be comprehensives (see, for example, Simon 1992; although Simon 1997 is more ambivalent). More broadly, too, as with earlier Labour governments he preferred to draw a contrast between the early expectations of change and the disappointments of office. With regard to Attlee's post-War Labour government, for example, he had already reminded himself to stress 'excitement and new hopes' following the General Election of 1945:

Get across the immediate post war (and post election) atmosphere rereconstruc-tion. Labour MPs return to Parliament and sing the Red Flag. Huge majority elected to a programme of social advance. . . . Among these was education,

where the Act had been passed towards the end of the war. Implications. . . . The
general context of educational change arising from the Act and elsewhere.

(Simon 1989)

These high hopes are then betrayed by 'manipulation and control', especially on the
part of officials at the new Ministry of Education: 'Thus, in spite of the hopes, surge
and planning behind the scenes positions were being strengthened against the forward, democratic movement. Role of the Ministry in all this. . . . Result. Growing
stagnation and stagnated hopes' (Simon 1989). Harold Wilson's Labour government
of the 1960s is likewise presented in ambivalent terms as one of high expectations
and limited results.

More generally, a key feature of Simon's interpretation of educational history is its
emphasis on the role of the State not as a benign or neutral umpire but as an active
and often undermining agent on behalf of class interests. His general argument was
that pressure for change came from the working class through its political representa-
tives, often rebuffed but never to be thwarted in the longer term. The State was not
to be trusted, whether in the guise of the Norwood committee which produced a
notorious rationalization of social inequalities in education during the Second World
War that helped to justify the so-called tripartite system of secondary schools in the
1940s and 1950s; or of Labour governments that failed to pursue the cause of comprehensive schools with sufficient vigour or commitment to thwart their many critics.
Although 'some working class leaders might accept Liberal ideas, and seek to climb
into the middle class themselves', he insisted that 'under the influence of the hard
facts of life the working-class movement would always rediscover its own needs and
take up the struggle for its own aims' (Simon 1960a, p. 367).

Conclusions

Simon succeeded brilliantly in producing a Marxist account that was a plausible way
of interpreting the development of education in England, as opposed to the liberal
pieties that had held the field in thrall for many years. This allowed him to portray the
Education Act of 1902, for example, in a very different way. The provision of state-
aided secondary education for a small academic minority, which the Act introduced,
was in his view at the expense of the educational interests of the majority of the
population (Simon 1965, p. 363). He was in many ways in the vanguard of the British
Marxist historians of the mid-twentieth century, for which he has not always been
given full credit (see, for example, Kaye 1984; Thompson *et al.* 1995). Simon's history
had a potent appeal because it spoke to contemporary debates and made sense in
these terms. It provided an explanation for social inequalities in education that could
no longer be ignored. It addressed the role of elite groups and individuals and of the
State itself that seemed to loom ever larger in the control of the education system.
It gave meaning to the many disappointments and failures of reform in education
over the past two centuries. And yet it also contrived to offer hope and inspiration
for the future, as Simon insisted that although 'periods of advance' were too often
followed by 'powerful and deliberate moves to turn back the clock', or else to 'direct

breakthroughs into innocuous channels', in the long run there would be a genuinely national system of education that met the needs of all (Simon 1998, p. 176). It was a persuasive analysis with a strong overarching theme.

Simon's contribution to the study of the history of education was immense, not only within Britain but also internationally. His ideas about the historical relationship between education and society developed still further the distinctive position of the history of education in Britain in helping to discredit the established liberal accounts. Moreover, his Marxist interpretation was produced several years before the 'radical revisionism' of Michael Katz and his colleagues began to dominate the field in the US. In terms of the history of education as a site of engagement between education, history and the social sciences, Simon's approach was one that emphasized the importance of politics within a critical Marxist framework of dialectical social and economic change. It rejected entirely the liberal model of gradual social progress, and posed a powerful claim for interpreting the relationship between education and social change as one that was based fundamentally on social class struggle. It provided also a means of engaging with sociologists and critical theorists, especially in the 1970s when many became increasingly pessimistic about the prospects of radical change. Despite all the setbacks, Simon insisted, history showed that success would eventually reward the educational struggles of the working-class movement, described on the final page of his fourth volume as

> the continuing endeavour to ensure access for all to a full, all-round education embodying humanist objectives and including science and technology – and conceived, one might add, in a generous spirit involving recognition of the full mystery of human potential.
>
> (Simon 1991, p. 558)

Inevitably, it was a contribution that was shaped by the social and political challenges of its own time, most notably the Cold War and inequality. Towards the end of the twentieth century and into the next there was growing interest in aspects of social inequality with which Simon himself had not been deeply concerned. One of these was gender inequality; as June Purvis complained, histories of education whether liberal or Marxist continued to emphasize the policies and experiences of men and boys, and to exclude from consideration those of women and girls (Purvis 1992). The inequalities experienced by other specific groups in society such as ethnic minority groups and refugees have also begun to be explored in greater depth (for example, Grosvenor 1997). In one sense this has increasingly required investigation of other aspects of social change over time that are not so bound up in notions of social class. Over 30 years ago, the sociologist Peter Musgrave was anxious that a dependence on social class as an analytical concept would undermine potential connections with other theoretical models, and might for this reason potentially stand in the way of relating the understanding gained in this specific field to general theories of social change. More particularly, Musgrave argued, 'This method fails to identify other important foci in the process of educational development and of social change' (Musgrave 1970, p. 15).

Since then, new research on gender differences, on the role of the family, on ethnicity, culture and national identity, on religion, on the experience of teaching and learning, on individual biography, and other areas has already done much to supersede a preoccupation with social class, with a recognition of a wide range of ways in which education has related to social change (see, for example, Goodman *et al.* 2009). Approaches to understanding the historical role of social class have themselves developed further, as, for example, the Australian historian of education Ian Davey suggested in the 1990s (Davey 1992). Historical attention has also tended to shift to the educational experiences of the middle classes as opposed to those of the working class (see McCulloch 2006). Nevertheless, in the context of his time, Simon made a unique and decisive contribution to interpreting the history of education, both as a scholar and as an activist, as part of a long term struggle for social equality.

5 The struggle for educational reform

A key purpose for the history of education has been to inform an understanding of the extensive educational reforms that have taken place in many countries, and to engage critically with these, with the aim of establishing a 'usable past'. Much of my own work has been concerned with attempting to relate historical analysis to contemporary policy developments. In this chapter I will rehearse the arguments that have sustained this approach, reflecting on its development over the past generation, and will then assess how far this has been effective and propose some lessons to be learned.

The test of time

Before the 1960s, the liberal emphasis on the gradual progress of education systems was reflected in many policy reports. It was a general perspective that was sympathetic to the official aims of education policy, and which was often employed to defend or rationalize particular policy developments. Although policy-oriented, it lacked a critical edge and awareness of the wider issues and interests that were involved. Thus, the version of the past at that time was usable because it was safe and domesticated. It provided a firm basis for shared values to be espoused and for existing developments to be continued.

Some products of this historical tradition were certainly informative and interesting, and exerted an important and in many ways beneficial influence on specific policies. In Britain, the Hadow Report on the education of the adolescent, published in 1926, announced with some confidence its recognition

> that in education, as in other departments of social policy, it is not possible to proceed *per saltum*, that no generation ever has a clean sheet on which to write, that each generation must build with materials inherited from the past on pain of not building at all.
>
> (Board of Education 1926, p. 77)

It continued in the course of a lengthy historical discussion of the provision of education for children of 11 to 15 years of age:

> As our survey shows, that problem has behind it a history extending back almost to the beginning of public education in England, and it has given rise,

particularly in recent years, to more fruitful educational activity. It is on the basis of the experience thus obtained that further progress will now be made. The question is not one of erecting a structure on a novel and untried pattern, but of following to their logical conclusion precedents clearly set, and of building on foundations which have long been laid.

(Board of Education 1926, p. 70)

Nevertheless, although the foundations that had been laid in the past were perceived to be fundamentally sound, they could still be responsible for difficulties that needed to be addressed in the present day.

The major cycle of education reform that took place in Britain in the 1940s, culminating in the 1944 Act, tended to adopt a radical stance rooted in this awareness of continuous development. The Spens Report on secondary education, published in 1938, had a strong sense of the importance of historical perspectives, and argued that:

> As we see one view or theory of education subjected to criticism and in consequence modified or superseded by another, we may be able partially to understand and appraise the value and meaning of each successive phase, and to form opinions of our own which, though they cannot possibly claim to be final, may at any rate claim to be based on something more substantial than current opinion and popular views of the significance of what has occurred.
>
> (Board of Education 1938, p. 1)

A further aspect of this was the Spens committee's awareness that its own expressed opinions 'cannot possibly claim to be final'. It realized that its ideas would eventually be 'subjected to criticism and in consequence modified or superseded' (Board of Education 1938, p. 1). Its historical awareness served as a warning that political fashions and social trends would continue to change, and that educational reforms needed to accommodate themselves to these.

Another feature of the educational reforms of the 1940s was that this historical consciousness was closely related to a sense of the social, cultural and philosophical goals of education. The Fleming report on the public schools, published in 1944, was keen to pursue a detailed historical account on the basis that 'the public schools, as living organisms with traditions in many cases lasting for centuries, can hardly be understood at all without some consideration of the past'. At the same time, and as part of this purpose, it attempted to come to terms with 'the social factors which have determined the development of these schools' (Board of Education 1944, pp. 5–6).

Spens developed a recognizably historical argument to support its proposed reforms, as did others at this time such as the Norwood report on the curriculum and examinations (Board of Education 1943) and the Fleming report on the public schools (Board of Education 1944; see also McCulloch 1994a). The President of the Board of Education R.A. Butler, himself a Conservative, could discuss the continuing importance of the Greek philosopher Plato with the socialist intellectuals G.D.H.

Cole and Harold Laski. As Butler recorded in what must have been a remarkable conversation in the offices of the Board of Education in 1942, 'Mr Cole and I discussed in an amiable manner what Plato had attempted to discuss before us, namely the best method of training the leaders of a community' (Butler 1942). Considering education in relation to broader issues immediately raised problems involving its social and historical development.

As I have previously argued, therefore (see McCulloch 1997a, 2000), during this period, roughly from the 1920s until the 1950s, a public history was incorporated and ingrained in state policy, validated by and contributing actively to it. This public history provided partial, selective, and often simplistic accounts of historical change that were designed for contemporary policy purposes. These accounts might be contested among competing groups and ideologies, for example, over the historical development of 'liberal' and 'vocational' approaches to education and the role of social class, but they helped to form the basis of widely shared collective values about the nature of education and the further development of the education system.

By the 1960s, this kind of partnership between policy and history was beginning to be undermined. In part, this was because the earlier confidence of gradual progress tended to be replaced by uncertainty as to the character and effects of past policies. The intimate relationship between history and policy that had been nurtured by liberal historians, based as it had been on shared values, hopes and interests, was ruptured to become one of mutual antagonism. The most prominent of the radical revisionists in the US, Michael Katz, led the way in arguing that there was no point in trying to reform the flawed institutions of schooling that had been inherited from the past, and indeed that it would be counter-productive to do so: 'Truly to reform we must conceive and build anew' (Katz 1968, p. 218). This type of history of education encouraged the development of critical scholarship in the field, but its value in engaging with educational policies was limited because of the mutual alienation and the lack of dialogue and shared sympathies that it tended to entail.

At the same time, the growing importance that was attached to education led to a preoccupation with educational reform on the part of national governments. This did not revive policy interest in the historical past, but rather engendered a focus on the future. The past came to be viewed negatively rather than in terms of providing solid foundations for further development. The past was the problem, to which the solution was the future. This hostile, negative image of educational history tended to mean that it was simplified and telescoped, used mainly to explain problems and failure. There also developed an ahistorical view of education reform as 'technical fix' (McCulloch 1995a). In this view, educational reform was a technical, managerial issue, concerned with addressing particular, narrowly defined problems, and was therefore seen as being unrelated to wider social, historical and cultural concerns. Reform also became subject to the imperatives of the electoral cycle to address perceived needs and problems, and increasingly to the media cycle to respond quickly to events. The considered and lengthy judgements of earlier policy reports were in these circumstances replaced by hurried and often poorly written proposals, by policies that rose without trace to appease a passing mood and win a friendly headline, and regularly reinvented the wheel.

1978). Such agencies would include the Treasury, and also professional and industrial organizations with their own vested interests and traditions. Warren continued that history, rather than being conducted on traditional lines, should instead be 'rigorously interdisciplinary', encouraging dialogue and engagement with economics, planning, administration and law. Warren also contended that in its approach to policy, history introduced a 'longitudinal' dimension, evoking the experience of past initiatives, to set against the more usual 'linear' tendency. Additionally, according to this view, it gave a stronger prospect of developing comparative policy studies, and accorded the humanities a greater role in a research area dominated by social and behavioural sciences. Warren concluded:

> Supplementing empirical data with qualitative assessments, history can bring to policy research the humanizing resources available to memory, ideas, values and traditions that join with grander economic, social, and political developments in shaping educational policies and determining their effects on people. History also can be useful in understanding the extent to which policy and policymaking are influenced by inertia, the weight of established practice, familiar ideas, and traditional approaches to problem solving. Within an interdisciplinary approach, history can liberate policy study from presentism.
>
> (Warren 1978, p. 16)

These suggestions offered clear guidelines for the practical implications of a history of education oriented towards contemporary policy.

Later contributions based in the US that examined the potential contributions of history to education policy often stressed the importance of being cautious in recommending change, avoiding reinventing the wheel, and providing better long-term planning (Lindemann 2000). Tyack and Cuban (1995), for example, advised that educational reform should go with the grain of teachers' cultures and what they called the grammar of schooling, but against the spin of simple, quick-fix solutions to deepseated dilemmas. They emphasized the continuities embodied in education, in the 'basic practices of schools' (ibid., p. 4). According to Tyack and Cuban, reforms were typically 'gradual and incremental', but although they might be criticized for being 'piecemeal and inadequate', nonetheless 'over long periods of time such revisions of practice, adapted to local contexts, . . . can substantially improve schools' (ibid., p. 5). They were also strongly critical of politicians and business leaders who failed to heed the lessons of history and lacked understanding of the social contributions of schools and the cyclical nature of policy, and persisted in 'pie-in-the-sky' hopes of transforming schooling through such devices as new technology or 'demonstration lighthouse schools' (ibid., p. 114). This increasingly negative note was also struck by authors such as Maris Vinovskis (1999).

In England, Charles Webster commented in 1976, just as the 'Great Debate' on education was being launched, that:

> It is only by reference to history that we will understand both the root causes of the present crisis of confidence, and the sources for our inegalitarian and heavily

bureaucratized educational system, and it is only by this means that we will be able to retrace the steps by which progress has been made at the cost of insensitivity to the cultural aspirations of the classes which the system was intended to serve.

(Webster 1976, p. 211)

Yet Webster added a warning at the same time: 'These are lessons which the bureaucrat and the politician are very unlikely to wish to learn' (Webster 1976, p. 211). The indifference and often hostility of policy makers to such inconvenient lessons of history was indeed to become a basic obstacle to promoting greater historical awareness in education policy. However, as Peter Gosden sagely observed,

> education as a field tends to be particularly attractive to those who see it as a means through which their own 'new' ideas might be deployed in order to make society 'more equal' or to 'support' industry or whatever other purpose may be receiving fleeting political and therefore official backing, regardless of past experience.
>
> (Gosden 1984, p. 7)

By contrast, Gosden preached a cautionary message about the excessive zeal of policy making conducted without a historical rudder, brake mechanism or rear-view mirror, and warned:

> Without some attention to the recent historical background – the collective memory of educational government – adequate evaluation of policy becomes impossible and avoidable blunders will be committed. Policy-makers will waste time and resources by tumbling into pitfalls with which they ought to be familiar and will spend their time trying to reinvent the wheel.
>
> (Gosden 1984, p. 7)

Harold Silver was especially prominent in advancing historical interpretations of recent and contemporary education policy. He complained that policy makers were increasingly regarding the future as 'liberation from a forgotten or forgettable past', concentrating on 'the straight line forward, not the tangled line back', leading to a 'public loss of history':

> Policy has become the overcoming of error so deep as to be best left ignored. Like the Americans at moments of crisis, we simply start again. . . . The most prominent historical references in official documentation tend to be to what ministers said or what government has said it wants.
>
> (Silver 1986).

In the world of policy, he added, 'the past is expunged, the present is disembodied, and the present is exhortation' (Silver 1986). Responding to issues raised by Conservative education policies in England in the 1980s, Silver argued that historical tools could help to penetrate 'current debate and policy, the processes, practices and vocabularies in which they are embodied, and which they reflect and engender' (Silver 1990, p. 1). Like Warren, Silver emphasized the need to relate closely to and be more involved in work in other disciplines, such as politics and social policy. Silver was especially interested in showing the policy process as it takes form over time, to explain how the assumptions, ideologies, opinions and interests that are involved in policy formation interact and change. Moreover, he was acutely conscious of the problematic aspects of seeking to relate history to policy, and of the likely effects of such an emphasis for historians themselves: 'In determining a proper role for themselves historians will be inevitably and usefully compelled to review their own organizing concepts and assumptions, to learn from evaluators, ethnographers and others grappling from different directions with the same complex sequences and processes' (ibid., p. 30).

Aspirations to promote stronger links between history and policy in education might therefore be interpreted as seeking to combine the policy concerns of the earlier liberal historians with the critical scholarship developed more recently, in order to engage critically but constructively with the issues of educational policy as they emerge in the present. Such a view would imply a need to restore a dialogue between historians and policy makers, to seek a measure of influence, but also to maintain a sense of distance which permits historians to challenge the assumptions upon which contemporary policies rest. There was also an element of counseling caution, or as Richard Aldrich proposed 'emphasising the need above all to retain that which is good while seeking to improve that which is of less worth' (Aldrich 1997/2006, p. 34). In general, as Raymond Williams had argued, after all, 'We do not solve the critical questions by understanding the history, but still an adequate sense of the history, as opposed to the ordinary functional myths, is the basis of any useful approach' (Williams 1961, p. 213). This was an important and attractive prospectus for a project upon which historians of education could embark in the context of the reforms of the late twentieth century. In practice, it was fraught with difficulty.

The turbulent years

My own academic career has been spent during the long period of educational reform that was introduced in Britain by James Callaghan's so-called 'Great Debate' in 1976, given ideological force under the Conservative governments of the 1980s and 1990s, and then renewed by Tony Blair and New Labour since 1997. These might well be described as the 'turbulent years', as Kenneth Baker, who himself made a distinguished contribution to the turbulence, entitled his own memoirs (Baker 1993).

As has already been seen, this phase of reform has also been international and global in nature, and I was witness to a remarkable set of parallel reforms that took place in New Zealand in the late 1980s under the 'New Labour' government of David Lange. Some of my earliest work analysed contemporary policy developments in New Zealand. These were the Picot reforms, based on the Picot report, *Administering for Excellence* (Taskforce to review education administration, 1988; see also Openshaw 2009). Having observed at close hand (while on study leave in England) the Conservative government's plans for education reform taking shape during 1987–88, I was struck on my return to New Zealand by the need to compare and contrast these Antipodean reforms. In terms of the educational traditions of New Zealand itself, they appeared to abandon the liberal-progressive assumptions that had permeated the Currie report of 1962 (Commission on Education in New Zealand, 1962) and the subsequent Education Act of 1964 (see McCulloch 1988). It appeared that Lange's reforms were influenced by the 'New Right' ideas that were already influential elsewhere such as in Britain and the US, while also seeking to revitalize the criteria and objectives of public education that had been uppermost in the 1950s and 1960s. The Picot Report itself seemed reminiscent of the early stages of the 'Great Debate' in Britain under James Callaghan and Shirley Williams, rather than of Margaret Thatcher and Kenneth Baker. Yet it seemed likely to act as a prelude to and legitimation of further radical reforms, just as had occurred in Britain in the 1970s and 1980s. I left New Zealand in 1991 to return to Britain soon after a conservative National government had taken office and it proceeded to put more radical measures into place.

My early forays into historical policy studies in England were focused on technical education. I sought to understand the failed post-War introduction of secondary technical schools as a 'usable past' with potential significance for the present (McCulloch 1989). In particular, I argued, this was a recent historical experience that offered potential lessons for the Technical and Vocational Education Initiative (TVEI), launched in 1982, and the city technology colleges (CTCs), introduced in 1986. I proposed a threefold typology for interpreting the historical thinking that underlay these recent reforms. The first was policy as pathology, since the reforms rested largely on a hostile attitude to the character and social effects of the state education system. As I noted, Prime Minister Thatcher stated this clearly in her speech to the Conservative Party annual conference in October 1987. She argued here that education needed to become 'part of the answer to Britain's problems' rather than 'part of the cause'. It should also allow the nation to 'compete successfully in tomorrow's world', rather than unsuccessfully as it had tended to do. At another level, too, she declared, 'individual boys and girls' were being 'cheated of a sound start in life'. Their proper 'opportunity', the 'education they need – the education they deserve', was 'all too often snatched away from them by hard-left education authorities and extremist teachers'. For these reasons, she concluded, the government was taking steps to ensure higher standards, the mastery of basic skills, and greater parental choice (*Times Educational Supplement* 1987).

The second aspect of current policies that I discerned was policy as plagiarism. Although dismissive of the record of the past and seeking to emphasize the novelty of current changes, those responsible for these new reforms had appropriated without due acknowledgement ideas and inventions that were in some cases as old as state education itself. One example of this was the CTCs, which although promoted as a 'new choice of school' (Department of Education and Science 1986) were in reality the latest version of an approach to education that had been developed around the world for the previous 300 years. Technical institutions, widely varying in their precise characteristics and aims, had long represented an alternative or antidote to the classical, literary and academic traditions of Western education. Thus current policies which set much store by their claim to originality were in fact far from new.

Third, I suggested that Conservative policies in technical schooling owed much to amnesia. They showed an inability to learn from the many past initiatives in technical schooling that had been promoted in England over the past two centuries, from the mechanics' institutes through to the secondary technical schools. Such initiatives had failed for many reasons that were often complex in nature, including the problems of local and institutional implementation. In particular, the recent experience of the secondary technical schools appeared to have been almost wholly forgotten and expunged from consciousness. It seemed to me in conclusion that continued failure to pay attention to these might well weaken or damage current reform initiatives; the CTCs were indeed a classic illustration of the view that those who ignore the past are condemned to repeat it. I note if I may that the CTCs were quietly abandoned a few years later, while the TVEI fell victim to the demands of the new National Curriculum and was also wound up.

Since that time, I have had the privilege to present three professorial lectures at different universities which together provide something of a running commentary or Greek chorus on current reforms from a historical perspective. My first, at Lancaster University in 1993 (McCulloch 1995a), ruminated on the lessons of the 'class of 1944', and whether history could provide a form of education for the present. My view was that history was an indispensable guide, although it could mislead as well as inform. I argued that the interplay between past and present has a special resonance when dealing with educational issues. In particular, I proposed, the historical experience of the reforms that had led to the Education Act of 1944 had a potential bearing for the would-be reformers of the 1990s. The Government White Paper of 1992, *Choice and Diversity* (Department for Education 1992) had sought to distance itself from the reforms of the 1940s, claiming that these, and the issues of the 1950s and 1960s that arose from them, belonged to a 'different educational world' (ibid., paragraph 1.49).Yet according to *The Times* on the day after the publication of the White Paper, 'The pattern most likely to emerge is roughly comparable to that obtaining under the 1944 Act, prior to the comprehensive reorganization' (*The Times* 1992). I insisted as vigorously as I could that issues around 'parity of esteem' and the idea of education as a civic project could and should be pursued on the basis of a historical understanding.

My second inaugural lecture, at the University of Sheffield in 1995, tried to develop potential connections between the Education Act of 1944 and the new challenges of the twenty-first century (McCulloch 1995b). It examined the kinds of historical perspective that were ingrained in even the most historically unaware of policies. It then assessed the visions of the future that are incorporated into educational reforms. The approach of the twenty-first century seemed a new way of disregarding the past, since it appeared that the problems that had afflicted education in the nineteenth and twentieth centuries would somehow cease to exist after the year 2000 (McCulloch 1995b, p. 10; see also McCulloch 1997b). Cultural, social and historical issues could be dismissed as 'historical' in nature, or simply as 'out of date'. Compromise and failure were consigned to the past. In a literal sense, this tendency represented the triumph of hope over experience, a preference to trust in the virgin future, rather than to dwell on the sullied past.

My third and surely final strike of this kind was my professorial lecture as the inaugural Brian Simon Professor of History of Education at the Institute of Education, London, in 2004 (McCulloch 2004a). This lecture naturally emphasized the contribution and legacy of Brian Simon as a historian of education. It also took the opportunity to analyse some of the educational policies of the new Labour government from a historical perspective. I noted that the references made to the vision and policies of the 1940s and the ideals of the 1960s seemed still to lack rigour and understanding. The chief inspector of schools, David Bell, had recently celebrated the sixtieth anniversary of the 1944 Act with the declared aim of exploring its lasting legacy, and considering the extent to which the education system had met the challenges posed by this Act. This was promising, but his account was uncritical of the 'visionary thinking' of R.A. Butler and nostalgic for some features of school life at that time (Bell 2004). He had managed to ignore the research of a generation of historians of education on the character of the 1944 Act, which had shed a great deal of light on its failures and limitations, as well as on the problematic nature of its lasting contribution to education.

Hard times

In the last few years, further historical issues have been raised, first as the Conservative and Labour parties jockeyed for advantage on educational reform prior to an impending general election, and second as an economic recession threatened to undermine any advances made in education over the previous decades. These recent developments provide some opportunity to peer forward into uncertain times, and at the challenges for educational reform in hard times, on which a historical perspective can offer some insight.

Tony Blair's Labour government after 1997 if anything increased the frenetic pace of educational reform inherited from the Conservatives. Well known for his emphasis on 'education, education, education', Blair presided over an era of policy neurosis, of policies announced, contradicted and discarded with unprecedented speed. Reforms were often 'gone before you know it', as in the case of the Education Action Zones (Franklin 2005). Like the Conservative reforms, they reflected a concern to limit the freedom that had previously been allowed to teachers and other educational professionals. In the case of schools, this constrained teachers especially in the curriculum domain, although under the banner of a 'new professionalism' (McCulloch 2001). In higher education, research, for example, came increasingly under the purview of the State (McCulloch 2003).

Despite this attention, and the increased financial resources that followed, a number of critics have recently talked about a 'failed generation' of children, blaming the Labour governments since 1997 for the disappointments of educational reform. Perhaps it was Unicef that effectively started this debate, with a report published in February 2007 that declared Britain to be the worst place in the industrialized world in which to grow up (Unicef 2007). But the Conservative Opposition was quick to seize the moment. According to George Osborne, the Shadow Chancellor of the Exchequer, 'This report tells the truth about [Gordon] Brown's Britain. After ten years of his welfare and education policies, our children today have the lowest well-being in the developed world' Brown, he argued, had 'failed this generation of children and will fail the next if he's given a chance' (Osborne 2007). In August 2007, the Conservative leader, David Cameron, argued that the Labour government was responsible for the rise of a 'yob culture', pointing out that many of today's 'yobs' were just five years old when Labour had come to power in 1997, and concluding: 'What I am determined, is that we are not going to fail another generation' (*Daily Telegraph* 2007). In April 2008, it was the turn of the Bow Group, a right wing think tank, that claimed in a new report entitled 'The Failed Generation: the real cost of education under Labour', that an 'entire generation' of schoolchildren had been let down by the Labour government (Skidmore 2008; see also *Daily Mail* 2008).

A fresh assault was launched in August 2008, as Michael Gove, the shadow Secretary of State for children, schools and families, published a further document under the title 'A Failed Generation: Educational Inequality under Labour'. The generation that was just completing its schooling, he averred, was a 'wasted generation'. 'Pupils taking their GCSEs this year were four when Labour came to power. Despite the government's promise to focus upon "education, education, education", millions of pupils have left school with little to show for their education, during a decade of persistent failure' (Gove 2008, p. 10).

Researchers based at the Institute of Education, Ruth Lupton and Natalie Heath, responded effectively to many of the points in the Conservative charge-sheet with a comprehensive statistical analysis (Lupton and Heath 2008), and this created an interesting though fairly brief public debate (Crace 2008). But what can historians of education bring to this discussion? There are two points that can be made first of all. First, if this is a failed generation, it might be added to a long list of them. We could say without too much exaggeration that there have been nearly 150 years of failures since the Elementary Education Act of 1870 first tried to 'fill the gaps' left by private educational provision. Some groups have been fairly well served over that time, but with the help of private schools which have been independent and largely separate from the efforts made by the State throughout that period. When Labour came to power in 1997 it was correct to argue in its first White Paper on education, *Excellence in Schools* (Department for Education 1997) that in this country a comparatively small elite had been well catered for, while the majority had been much less well served; and that this basic characteristic had what it called 'deep and historic roots' in that, unlike in many other countries, mass education was provided only grudgingly at the end of the nineteenth century and was only slowly acknowledged as being important during the twentieth century. Working-class children were consistently failed, for example, in a number of state experiments with different kinds of school, with the post-Second World War experiment of secondary modern schools one of the most spectacularly unsuccessful of these, based on a pious hope of 'parity of esteem' between different types of school that also failed to flourish when put to the test (McCulloch 1998a). Against this long historical record, the modest gains of the last ten years assume their true significance. They are not altogether surprising, for they are pitched against the grain of deep-seated cultural values and social interests.

A second kind of framework that a historian might wish to propose is that a 'failed generation' could refer just as well to a failed generation of educational reform. This could address the past 30 years and more of education policy initiatives. The centrepiece, even in a crowded landscape, was undoubtedly Baker's Education Reform Act of 1988. Ideologically, as John Patten's White Paper of 1992, *Choice and Diversity* (Department for Education 1992), took pains to point out, the five 'great themes' of the 1980s continued to be dominant and pervasive: quality, diversity, parental choice, greater autonomy for schools and greater accountability. Underlying much of this was a notion of a free market in education that mirrored the economic aspirations of the time. In some ways educational reform has moved on from the debates of the late 1980s, but still they have left their mark in powerful ways and have left a profound legacy in our education system and thinking. It was of course the Conservative governments of Margaret Thatcher and John Major that dominated these debates. A failure to recognize that this made a fundamental contribution to our recent education reforms is surely a rather sad example of historical amnesia. Another aspect of this was the initiative by Lord (formerly Kenneth) Baker to promote 'university technical schools', highlighting the loss of the postwar technical schools but with little reference to the failed reforms in the 1980s of the TVEI and his own CTCs (*The Guardian* 2009).

Thus, some of the critiques of Labour's educational reforms show a certain lack of historical awareness. Yet this historical amnesia is also consistent with the past generation of educational reform, relieved only by the odd flash of recognition. The most recent policy initiatives have shown a tendency to overlook the earlier phases of reform, for example the developments in the post-14 vocational curriculum of the last few years trying hard to forget the TVEI of the 1980s; just as the progenitors of the TVEI and CTCs chose to forget the lessons of the postwar secondary technical schools. Similarly, the initiative by the Labour government to raise the participation age of education to 18 has shown only the dimmest recollection of previous attempts, for example, the long debate about raising the school leaving age from 15 to 16 that occupied the 1960s and early 1970s.

Meanwhile, the familiar terms of debate seem to have been altered, the times have changed, and the stakes are raised. The global credit crisis, together with the rise in international tensions and conflicts, appears to presage hard times ahead. If history is important for underpinning and understanding educational reform, it has a starker and even greater role when times are hard.

Two examples may help to develop this point. First, economic hardship often leads to cuts in educational expenditure, and indeed often it is education that is the first area to suffer. If we look back to the 1920s and 1930s, we can see this very strikingly. In Britain, Brian Simon's *Politics of Educational Reform* demonstrates the preoccupation with 'economy' and the social effects of this (Simon 1974). The so-called 'Geddes Axe' of 1922, for example, proposed cuts of £18 million from the estimates for education, raising the age of entry to school from five to six, increasing class sizes, reducing teachers' salaries and pensions, cutting back on free places to secondary schools and on the development of junior technical and day continuation schools, and reducing the numbers of teachers in training. Over the medium term, Simon concludes: 'In the memory of those who lived through them, the inter-war years were dominated by the cry for, and practise of, economy. In the elementary schools especially expenditure was cut to the bone, everything done on the cheap' (Simon 1974, p. 294). This became what Simon describes as a 'way of life', in which

> Children must ease themselves into outworn desks of the wrong size and nailed to the floor, in classrooms with high windows obscuring any view, make their way into backyards to find insanitary earth closets, seek out the nearest park to find a blade of grass, travel to find a distant playing field – or, if that were impossible, do without, though within the school there was no aid to physical training either.
>
> (Simon 1974, p. 295)

If we look to the US of that period, such privations come across, if anything, even more clearly. Some years ago, the US educational historians Tyack, Lowe and Hansot produced an excellent book entitled *Public Schools in Hard Times: The Great Depression and Recent Years* (Tyack, Lowe and Hansot 1984). In this, they investigated the relationship between education and what they called the 'politics of money'. In particular, they explored the schools of the 1930s, 'behind the schoolhouse door', to 'recapture the daily experience, the perplexity, of diverse Americans living through those "years of the locust"'. They also attempted to analyse the depression decade from a distance, 'raising questions about how public schooling in the 1930s appears in the longer trajectory of twentieth-century history', and comparing it with more recent years.

A collection of articles on this topic has also been produced which very interestingly attempts to understand the Great Depression as world history, in which 'common responses by different governments facing similar conditions produced undesirable outcomes that exacerbated the economic crisis'. It thereby 'places economic globalization, political instability, and curricular experimentation at the centre of analysis' (Ewing and Hicks 2006, p. 14). It also insists that this history 'remains significant in the contemporary world, as new processes of globalization and old structures of power, opportunity, and access continue to shape the meaning and experience of schooling nationally and internationally' (ibid.).

If one looks to more recent times, the 1960s, we can recall the consequences of devaluation of the pound under Harold Wilson's Labour government of 1967, for example, in Richard Crossman's graphic diary account of the Cabinet meeting of 16 November 1967 which postponed the raising of the school leaving age:

> As soon as Cabinet assembled this morning the Chancellor started reading aloud the details of his package – so much on hire purchase, bank rate, etc., £75 million cuts in public expenditure, abolition of domestic rate-payers' de-rating with a saving of £30 million and the postponement of the raising of the school leaving age. There was no Cabinet paper. Everything was announced verbally and so fast that there was only just time to write it down. When he'd finished I blew up. I said I'd never seen business done in such a deplorably incompetent way.
>
> (Crossman 1979, p. 405).

Here we see evoked so well the suddenness, the panic reaction, the feeling of things being out of control, the loss of established patterns; and education highly vulnerable in the middle of it all.

Secondly, we might reflect on the links between international turbulence and conflict on the one hand, and educational reform on the other. Sometimes there is a basic issue about how to keep educational services going at all, and the 'lost generation' has often had an altogether bleaker implication in such times. And yet there is also a hopeful note sounded here, because educational reform has often been stimulated by these kinds of international tensions. In Britain, the Boer War, the First World War and the Second World War all helped to promote radical ideas. Indeed in the Second World War it was the memory of the failed hopes of the First World War that helped reformers like R.H. Tawney to be even more determined to bring about reform through the 1944 Education Act. The lesson here might be that in hard times we try to protect our educational reforms and go on to make them more effective and meaningful; that history provides us with ample warnings of what happens when education is undermined at such times; and examples of how they can provide renewed hope and a vision for educational reform. It can help us to recognize the ideals and aspirations that have marked out the best of our educational reforms, and seek to renew these once again, in the good times, and also in the bad.

Conclusions

The role of the history of education in the struggle for educational reform has been contested and denied not only by policy makers, but also by a number of historians of education who prefer to avoid giving excessive attention to the present. Marc Depaepe has argued against a 'functionalist' approach which he attributes to 'frustration and anger' and 'a kind of corporatist defensive reflex' on the part of historians of education (Depaepe 2003, p. 189). Depaepe was particularly critical of an edited collection based at the Institute of Education, London (Crook and Aldrich 2000b), which emphasized a case for contributing to educational reform, going so far as to claim that it bore 'first and foremost the stamp of hackwork', and did no 'real service to the discipline' (Depaepe 2003, p. 191). My own contribution to this collection (McCulloch 2000) was dismissed as risking 'degenerating into an ahistorical supply firm of hidden political agendas – educational and otherwise' (Depaepe 2003, p. 189). Moreover, he continued, it needed to 'make the effort of looking over the wall of the painstakingly constructed borders of one's own discipline as well as those of one's own language and culture' (ibid., p. 190).

The risks that Depaepe describes are real, and many historians have similarly warned against 'sharpening contemporary axes' for simple solutions to current problems taken out of their due historical context (see, for example, Goodson 1988). Yet it seems no less valid to warn against the dangers of historians of education remaining in 'splendid isolation' in their own research specialisms without reference to present challenges and changes (ibid.). Moreover, historians of education are far from alone in seeking out historical contributions to current social and policy changes. The international historian Margaret MacMillan is merely the latest, if one of the most eloquent, to explore the role of history in general based on a rigorous approach to addressing current dilemmas (MacMillan 2009; see also Reisz 2009).

As will be apparent, I have never agreed with those historians of education who would argue that the present day is none of their concern. Much of the best educational history has illuminated both the past and the present. My own notion of a usable past, as for the other historians mentioned already, is much more about a grown up conversation, aware of contradictions and complexities, prepared to confront problems and doubts and to address them openly, than about an instrumental, functional and prescriptive set of lessons. Nor would I wish to present myself as a fount of all knowledge and wisdom about the future. Historical interpretations are themselves contested and debated. I would simply argue that historical voices are of value for current debates, and that they have tended to be neglected over the past generation.

It is a serious concern that 30 years of educational reform have shown such little regard for the advice of historians of education. As David Raffe and Ken Spours have recently argued, there has been a continued unwillingness to learn. They suggest that reforms in 14–19 education have suffered because of a failure to learn from the past, yet that such learning is still capable of improving reform in the future. According to Raffe and Spours, over the last 25 years, each policy innovation in this area has seemed to fail to learn from the experience of previous innovations, while at the same time 'this inability or unwillingness to learn from the past has been accompanied by superficial learning from the experience of other countries', as governments borrowed policy ideas from abroad, 'with little regard to differences of culture or context and with a tendency to borrow from the countries which suited the political mood rather than those which had relevant experience to share' (Raffe and Spours 2007, p. 2). This chapter has made a more generalized case in the same broad spirit. There have been calls for a 'new education debate', aiming to build on the educational developments that have come about since the 'Great Debate' of 1976 (Seldon 2010). It must be hoped that such a debate would reflect critically and in a historically informed way on the nature of the educational reforms themselves.

It remains a legitimate and worthy purpose for the history of education to struggle for educational reform. As a project, it has been consistent with other key projects in the history of education in seeking a broad purpose and underlying dynamic. Nevertheless, it must be conceded that this has proved to be a largely thankless and often dispiriting task. Webster was correct to predict in 1976 that bureaucrats and politicians would be unwilling to learn inconvenient historical lessons. The general indifference to the issues raised has also created anxieties over the significance and relevance of the history of education as a field. The causes for which it had fought for over a century were being played out to a diminishing audience. The search was on for fresh ideas and new directions.

6   The struggle for theory and methodology

In a widely noted paper published in 1999, Jurgen Herbst, a distinguished and experienced international historian of education, and a former president of the History of Education Society in the US and also the International Standing Conference for the History of Education, delivered a stinging critique of contemporary trends in the field. According to Herbst, the theoretical and methodological concerns of the history of education, so fresh a generation earlier, had now become stale and repetitive. In the 1960s, he suggested, the 'revisionist' approach to the history of education, which he associated with the American historians Bernard Bailyn and Lawrence Cremin, had revitalized interest and created new agendas. The educational histories of the 1960s pursued fresh themes, but 'did not feel bound by any orthodoxy of ideology, subject, or historical methodology' (Herbst 1999, p. 738). They could be conservatives, liberals or radicals; they could employ a wide range of methodologies from traditional historical narratives, to analytical social science, to quantitative methodologies, to theoretical discussions. They were also able to study education in its widest sense and in many different settings, not only as it has been experienced in school and during childhood and youth, but throughout life and society. By contrast, he complained, at the turn of the twenty-first century the history of education was stale and repetitive, with little 'genuine fresh input'. Indeed, he emphasized, 'Most writings tend to fill gaps in the record or bring to our attention groups or issues that have been overlooked in the past' (ibid., p. 739). Herbst continued:

> We endlessly repeat old mantras . . . class, race, and gender being the one [sic] most often heard – but we are no longer sure just where and how we are to apply them. They seem like empty formulae waiting to be filled with new subject matter. The best we seem able to do is, following the currently fashionable trend of identity politics, perfunctorily to reach for another topic, another subject, and hope that it will fit the pre-set mold.
>
> (Herbst 1999, p. 739)

Overall, Herbst concluded, the history of education as a field had lost the intellectual vitality that would make it possible for it to make a strong contribution in the changed conditions of the twenty-first century.

Herbst's critique provides a somewhat idealized and nostalgic view of the 1960s, and a bleak and pessimistic prognosis for the present. It constitutes a profound and significant challenge to the views of other historians of education who have argued that the history of education is currently in a healthy and vigorous condition. Roy Lowe, for example, has suggested that since the early 1960s, over the span of his own professional career, 'the writing of the History of Education has undergone little short of a revolution' (Lowe 2000, vol. I, p. xlii). According to this view, the reaction against the earlier Whiggish and 'Acts and facts' types of history has been fully sustained since the 1960s. Thus, for Lowe,

> In recent years, History of Education has become clearly identified as a full and proper element in the study of history more generally, with a central role to play in the development of social, economic and political history, and this development can be only for the good.
>
> (Lowe 2000, vol. I, p. xliii)

This general view is endorsed by Crook and Aldrich, who insist that in terms of research and publications, 'British history of education entered the twenty-first century in a relatively strong position' (Crook and Aldrich 2000a, p. x). A detailed review of British published research in the field concurs that it is producing 'excellent, core research' (Race 2004, p. 320), and adds for good measure that it 'can influence education policy debates in both national and international contexts' (ibid.).

This chapter argues in response to Herbst that the field can benefit through a critical engagement with the theories and methodologies of the broader humanities and social sciences, and that this process has already begun to be evident in recent work. In some respects these new approaches are addressing significant underlying features of the field that were not confronted, or perhaps even clearly understood, during the twentieth century. Historians of education are finding new ways of engaging with theoretical and methodological problems, and applying these to specific areas of study. In particular, there are interesting possibilities being found for recasting the terms of debate within which the history of education has usually been framed. I will examine first of all the nature of the engagement between theory and the history of education, in particular its position in relation to 'empiricist' and 'postmodernist' positions which have been especially challenging for the field. I will then address the ways in which historians of education have begun to seek fresh methodological approaches.

History and theory

The history of education has faced two closely related problems in its relationship with theory, one general and the other more specific. The first of these has been the broad issue of identifying theoretical frameworks within which to locate historical accounts. The second has been the challenge posed by postmodernists and other critics who have accused the history of education of being 'empiricist' in nature. These are problems that history as a whole has needed to confront over the past 30 years. They have been particularly acute in the case of the history of education, and especially challenging to resolve.

History as a discipline has often had the reputation of not engaging with philosophy and theory. Historians have actually been rather reticent about discussing such matters; as Fritz Stern noted in introducing the varieties of history since the nineteenth century, 'most historians seem reluctant to articulate their views about history' (Stern 1956a, p. 15). Stern continued:

> The one time when historians seem to be willing to overcome their reluctance is when they are being attacked or are themselves attacking prevailing forms of historiography. Mostly, however, they prefer to let their finished work testify for them, and as to theory content themselves with occasional asides, usually in letters.
>
> (Stern 1956a, p. 15)

The sociologist C. Wright Mills also observed that although history was highly theoretical in its nature, many historians displayed a 'calm unawareness' of this that he found impressive but unsettling. According to Mills, the historian cannot avoid interpretation and selection in seeking an understanding of the past, 'although he may attempt to disclaim it by keeping his interpretations slim and circumspect' (Mills 1959, p. 145). There is something of a taboo surrounding such issues that is part and parcel of the modern historical profession. Nevertheless, since the late twentieth century historians have again needed to respond to challenges and attacks from outside.

These recent criticisms of history have arisen in particular from its established tendencies from the nineteenth century onwards (referred to previously in Chapter 2) to be positivistic and quasi-scientific in its approach in a manner that has often been labeled as empiricist. Postmodernists and other critics have questioned whether it is possible to understand the past in these terms and proposed that familiar ideas about historical causation and influence, long taken for granted by historians, are inherently problematic (see, for example, Spiegel 2005). Some have been attracted by the opposite view that different readings of the past are equally valid, which tends, as Richard Evans has noted, to lend itself to a relativist claim that 'in the end no kind of objective knowledge about the past, in the sense of the patterns of interconnectedness that makes it history rather than chronicle, can ever be possible' (Evans 1997, p. 231). At its most extreme, this is reflected in Alan Bennett's play *The History Boys*, with the young teacher Irwin convincing his pupils that 'for the purposes of this examination truth is, if not an irrelevance, then so relative as just to amount to another point of view', albeit that this argument comes to grief on the reality of the Holocaust in the Second World War (Bennett 2004, p. 73). In these circumstances a number of historians like Evans have felt obliged to overcome their professional reticence and respond to such criticisms. In so doing, they have often reflected more broadly on the general relationship between history and theory. The distinguished cultural historian Peter Burke, for example, has suggested that a convergence has taken place between historians on the one hand and theorists on the other, in 'an age of blurred lines and open intellectual frontiers, an age at once exciting and confusing' (Burke 2005, p. 19).

The history of education as a field of study has reflected many of these debates and tensions. Yet, as Harold Silver has justly observed, 'A sensitive dialogue between the historical evaluation of experience, and the intrusive nature of theory, has never been more necessary' (Silver 1983, p. 241). Mark Olssen has also insisted that 'the historian of education of education must see himself/herself as being necessarily involved in a theory-bound enterprise, and that they must take cognizance of the theoretical tools and concepts and assumptions that are viewed as progressive' (Olssen 1987, p. 38). A useful example of such work is the approach taken by Pavla Miller, who has insisted that 'consciously or not, historians employ a range of conceptualizations of the state in their work' (Miller 1989, p. 302), and that they need to clarify concepts that under-pin debates about the historiography of compulsory schooling. According to Miller,

> If historians are informed about significant theoretical issues, they can not only employ up-to-date theory in their own writing, but resolve some of the theoretical puzzles which only empirical research can address. Moreover, the histories of schooling might contain some essential pieces of the complex jigsaw linking class and gender relations.
>
> (Miller 1989, p. 303)

In assessing the interactions between the labour movement, family economies, gender, class and age relations, demography, and compulsory schooling, Miller concluded, 'historians of education are likely to find themselves in the thick of theoretical debates' (Miller 1989, p. 303).

Attempts have been made to 'bridge the gap' between history and theory in education, for example between the history and philosophy of education, and indeed Depaepe has argued forcefully that 'in spite of the large gulf between the philosophy and the history of education, from the perspective of the sociology of science, a relationship, in content, still continues to exist' (Depaepe 2007, p. 39). Nevertheless, it is clear that there continue to be mutual misunderstandings (Standish 2008). Moreover, the difficulties over theory in general and empiricism in particular have been especially profound in the case of the history of education because of the 'Acts and facts' approach with which it was associated for much of the twentieth century. It is this that has given the field an enduring reputation for being dominated by an empiricist outlook. One critic, Kevin Brehony, has contended: 'The preferred mode of research and writing in History of Education has remained resolutely empiricist and marked by a disdain for social theory' (Brehony 2003, p. 441). Kevin Myers has recently singled out the history of education in England as remaining 'predominantly empiricist' (Myers 2009, p. 804).

Over the past 20 years, postmodernist approaches have become prominent in some circles in the history of education, and it may be that this in itself is because of a reaction against the extremes of 'Acts-and-facts' history. Thus, for instance, Sol Cohen has pursued the implications of a 'linguistic turn' in the history of education (Cohen 1999). He does not assert a wholly relatively relativist position, in that he concedes that we may believe in 'the historical real, in a recuperable past, in objectivity as an ideal to strive for, and in historical writing as a medium for truthful representation', but he argues that 'the difference between history and literature, the historian and the novelist, may be narrower than we have been accustomed to think' (Cohen 2003a, p. 319).

The history of education thus faces a significant challenge in needing both to assess in general terms how to develop an engagement with theory, and also to respond to the specific intellectual challenge posed by postmodernist arguments. In relation to theoretical engagement as a general issue, I have previously noted, with Ruth Watts, that it is most important to resist any temptation that there may be to retreat or withdraw from such concerns, or to revert to the isolationism of chronological and descriptive approaches (McCulloch and Watts 2003). It also means much more than a grudging recognition of these broader discussions. It entails in addition exhibiting sensitivity to the potential use of different theories in enhancing our understanding of the historical past. Here there are still uncharted possibilities in the humanities and social sciences more generally that promise a great deal, and to which renewed attention may be given.

In doing so, historians of education should strive to learn from the insights developed in social scientific theory (see also, for example, Davey 1987). It is also no less necessary to be critical and sceptical of the theories themselves, as opposed to applying them uncritically or indiscriminately. Moreover, it is important to avoid applying theory in a 'prefabricated' way, that is, prior to engaging in historical analysis. Clarence Karier, in the US, has proposed that social theory should emerge in a 'transactional relationship' with historical inquiry, in that, as he argues,

> Fully developed theory ought to be a consequence of historical inquiry, not a prerequisite. The consequences of prefabricated theories . . . placed on a given historical experience, can and often do carry a heavy tendency to distort the world of the historical actor.
>
> (Karier 1979, p. 165)

This would not be a novel development in itself; as has been demonstrated in earlier chapters, there has been a great deal of interaction between the history of education and social theories of different kinds. Articulating and reflecting on this relationship in an explicit manner has however been far from a consistent practice, and this is a matter that needs and deserves constant vigilance.

In seeking to respond to the specific challenge of postmodernist theory, there have been significant attempts to highlight the importance of seeking after historical truth. Richard Aldrich, for example, argues that this is nothing less than a duty for the historian of education, introducing a note of ethical concern to the debate. Aldrich challenges the relativist tendencies of much postmodernism, and insists that there were realities in the past, for once they were the realities of the present, although he also acknowledges that 'most historians would acknowledge that their work is of a hypothetical or tentative nature, and few are unaware of the difficulties of the task' (Aldrich 2003, p. 140). As he concludes,

> Across the centuries historians have acknowledged the partial nature of their enterprise and the impossibility of complete capture of the past, and yet have

continued to search for ways of representing segments of it as accurately or as provocatively as possible.

(Aldrich 2003, pp. 141–42)

Further to such reflections, there may also be opportunities to challenge the rigid dichotomy often posed between 'naïve realism' of the Acts and facts type, on the one hand, and relativism on the other. Michael Young's recent work has proposed what he describes as a 'social realist' approach to knowledge which includes recognizing an element of objectivity and truth in social relations. The sociology of education, he argues, needs 'to develop a theory of knowledge that, while accepting that knowledge is always a social and historical product, avoids the slide into relativism and perspectivism with which this insight is associated in postmodernist writings' (Young 2008, p. 19). This raises profound epistemological and ontological issues that should also be relevant to the history of education.

Other discussions of reality and theory in the history of education were, like Aldrich's, included in a special issue of *History of Education* on theory and methodology that was also linked to a very successful and well attended symposium held in 2003 at the annual conference of the American Educational Research Association. A paper by myself, for example, explored the problems of 'virtual history', or 'might-have-been' history, in the history of education, arguing that this amounted in many cases to unverifiable speculation and indeed retrospective wishful thinking (McCulloch 2003b; see also, for example, Hawthorn 1991; Ferguson 1997). Joyce Goodman explored the potential of Walter Benjamin's ideas about 'montage' to raise questions about nineteenth-century women educationists and their deployment of languages of 'active citizenship' (Goodman 2003). Benjamin uses a dialectical image of reality to link people and experiences, and moments and discontinuities, juxtaposing images dialectically, and Goodman argued that, like gender, his approach might help to foster new insights for both histories and theories of education, and for the relationship between them (ibid., p. 174). Also in this set of papers, Derrick Armstrong studied the significance of philosophical idealism and the methodology of 'voice' in the history of education, seeking to work beyond the ideas of E.G. Collingwood and Walter Oakeshott about historians' reconstructions of the past, and focusing on the contributions made by the pragmatist philosophy of Pierce, James and Dewey (Armstrong, D. 2003). Armstrong's essay most interestingly repositions life histories as a means not merely of illuminating small-scale events but rather of achieving 'the theorization, historically, of the relationships between structure and agency, policy and experience, power and resistance' (ibid., p. 217).

Some Marxists have been attracted to what might be described as a neo-realist approach especially because of its emphasis on structure and transformation. Gregor McLennan asserts that 'a realist conception of explanation can assist both the empirical moment in historiography and its theoretical structure' (McLennan 1981, pp. 235–36), and that it can thus support a Marxist approach to history. He is drawn to realist accounts to counter both empiricist and relativist conceptions of history. This is also the case for the sociologist George Steinmetz, who has examined a range of positions from 'relativist discursivism' to 'hard headed positivism' and suggests that 'The explanatory practice of most historical social scientists is best captured by the philosophy of science position known as critical realism' (Steinmetz 1998, pp. 170–71). Indeed, according to Steinmetz, positivists, theoretical realists and conventional idealists, whatever their disagreements with each other, concur that most historical social scientists are methodologically flawed in their approach: 'either they are too scientific or not scientific enough, too wedded to the notion of explanation or to an indefensible form of explanation'. However, Steinmetz proposes, it is the historians' preference for 'multicausal, contingency-based' approaches that is the most appropriate for 'capturing the ontological specificity of social reality' (ibid., p. 174). In his view, it is critical realism that offers the best way into these approaches, as he concludes: 'Critical realism allows us to safely steer between the Scylla of constricting definitions of science and the Charybdis of solipsistic relativism' (ibid., p. 184; see also Steinmetz 2005).

Some recent analyses of educational change that combine historical inquiry with sociological theory have begun to move in this direction. In different ways, these have found new directions in unsettling relationships between individual lives and the wider society, and between agency and structure, both challenging neat and straightforward dualisms and also rejecting smooth transitions between them. This includes work by Margaret Archer, well known in the history of education and comparative education for her key contributions on the social origins of educational systems, in relation to structure and agency, subjectivity and objectivity, and the importance of recognizing them as irreducible to each other (Archer 2007). Tone Skinningsrud, in Norway, has also investigated the.dislocations between education and social change, in particular through an examination of the relationship of the emergent educational structure with other agencies such as the church and the state (Skinningsrud 2005; see also Scott 2000, Maton 2010).

Clearly there is a rich and continuing epistemological debate being pursued in the social sciences around the social relationships of knowledge. Historians of education should be able to take part in this argument and assume different positions within it, while making use of it to enhance their understanding of the historical past. The recent emergence of neo-realist viewpoints also raises the possibility that the history of education may be able to find a middle way between the polar opposites of empiricism and relativism that have tended to undermine it in the past.

Methodology and the history of education

Earlier research in the history of education tended to privilege the administration of education systems, and more recently policy making in education from the viewpoints of the policy makers. As Derrick Armstrong has noted, for example, 'The voices of those who have made policy through government committees and reports and of those professionals who have implemented and sometimes contested these policies tend to dominate' (Armstrong, D. 2003, p. 201). This was a 'top-down' approach to the history of education that was characteristic not only of liberal accounts of social progress, but also of the more radical interpretations of social change and conflict that sought to supersede them.

This top-down tendency was in part due to the characteristic method that was employed in the history of education. This was to examine the surviving documents left by the administrators, policy makers, politicians and head teachers who led organized national systems of schooling. These generally consisted of published policy reports, speeches, and articles and books produced by these leading individuals, together with commentaries drawn from newspapers and journals. The history of education therefore tended to be viewed through the eyes of the 'winners' of conflicts over the nature and purposes of education (see also McCulloch and Richardson 2000, p. 115). This kind of historical evidence also said little about many of the groups involved in education. As Phil Gardner pointed out, 'when we leave the well-illuminated world of policy and political personalities, our knowledge falls away'. Indeed, according to Gardner, 'We know little of how the changing educational landscape was perceived and accommodated by those who were to be most affected by it – by children, by parents and, in particular, by teachers' (Gardner 1996, p. 237).

For the same reasons, working–class children, girls and women, the disabled, ethnic minorities and indigenous peoples were marginalized and even excluded from the history of education. Stephen Humphries argued in his major work *Hooligans or Rebels?* (Humphries 1981) that working-class youth were generally portrayed as 'hooligans' in official documents, while their 'resistance' to the dominant culture and the structures that oppressed them was 'under-recorded and under-researched' (ibid., p. 3). Even earlier, Joan Burstyn pointed out from a review of the literature on women's education in England in the nineteenth century that 'women seldom appear in the sources traditionally defined as historically important' (Burstyn 1977, p. 11). In the last few years, historians of education have also noted that disability and disabled people are under-represented in the history of education, and have been critical of the methods adopted in earlier work. Felicity Armstrong, for example, observed of one prominent work, D.G. Pritchard's *Education and the Handicapped, 1760–1969* (Pritchard 1963) that its dependence on such sources as official reports and conference proceedings neglected key aspects of the lives and experiences of the disabled (Armstrong, F. 2007, p. 553). Similarly, Kevin Myers complains about the prevailing historical silence around ethnic minority and immigrant groups in Europe, and also attributes this in part at least to these resilient methodological traits in the field (Myers 2009). There has been a widespread view, too, that historical work by concentrating on official policy reports and records has left the lives and experiences of indigenous people out of the account in many countries around the world (see, for example, Timutimu *et al.* 1998; Denzin *et al.* 2008).

Further to this, concentrating on particular kinds of documentary source also meant a failure to engage with the history of the classroom and the teaching-learning interface. In the early 1980s, Harold Silver pointed out that histories of education concerned with Victorian England had focused on policy formation, legislation, commissions, committees, the provision, control and administration of education, and the changing shape of different levels of education, while they had neglected relationships within schools. Indeed, he concluded, 'There are no published studies of possible varieties of educational experience in monitorial schools, workhouse schools, factory schools, dame schools – indeed all schools' (Silver 1983, p. 22).

Increasingly, these lacunae in the history of education have been addressed through recourse to new methodological approaches. In part, this has involved making use of a broader range of documentary evidence, as well as asking different questions of the more familiar sources. It has also meant engaging with oral history, visual history, sensory history, and materiality in history.

The broadening range of documentary source material that historians of education are now enlisting includes personal documents such as letters, diaries and autobiographies (see McCulloch 2004b and McCulloch 2011 for more detailed overviews of documentary research in education). These kinds of documents have facilitated study not only of biographical and personal dimensions in the history of education, but also of dynamic relationships between the private and public realms of education over the longer term. A biographical turn in the field was strongly influenced by feminist theory and politics. These raised significant methodological concerns such as,

> the nature of historical evidence, the need to uncover the forgotten stories of women as teachers, the material conditions of teaching as work for women, and the ways that the framing of gender and sexuality has shaped women's and men's experience in the educational state.
>
> (Weiler and Middleton 1999, p. 2)

One instance of research that takes this approach is that of James Daybell, who has examined letters written and sent by women in Tudor England as evidence of female education and literacy at that time. As Daybell notes, because most women were taught within the household or the Church, relatively few documentary sources had survived. Nevertheless, according to Daybell, women's letters from that period constitute unique evidence not only of basic writing activity and abilities, but also of more advanced forms of female literacy such as the ownership and reading of books, knowledge of classical literature, and interest in music, poetry and other intellectual pursuits (Daybell 2005, p. 695). He points out, indeed, that over 10,000 individual letters sent by women in England, Wales, Scotland and Ireland before 1642 are still in existence in various locations, and that for the period between 1540 and 1603 alone a comprehensive search has unearthed over 3,000 manuscript letters sent by over 650 individual women (ibid., p. 698). In other cases, the study of letters has been combined with an interest in other personal documents. Tanya Fitzgerald, for example, has focused on the letters and diaries of Church Missionary Society women teachers at the Paihia mission station in Aotearoa/New Zealand between 1823 and 1835, which she describes as 'needles in the haystacks of male prose' (Fitzgerald 2005, p. 658). According to Fitzgerald, '"Home" as a form of archive is not an impossibility, particularly as the "archive" originated from the storage of public records in a private space' (ibid., p. 660).

At the institutional level, textbooks, school magazines, school books and log books have become familiar sources not only for the detailed information that they provide on the curriculum and other features of life in schools and other educational organizations, but also for the values and interests represented through these textual devices. The literary historians Evelyn Arizpe and Morag Styles have documented children's experiences of text in the 1740s, 'learning to decode not only letters, words and visual designs, but also the social, cultural and moral values upheld by their mother' (Arizpe and Styles 2004, p. 337). Elsewhere, Irish national school books have been examined for the ideals that they articulated in the Irish system of national schools and also for their ideological purchase in schools in Ontario, Canada following their importation from the 1850s onwards (Walsh 2008). School log books may also be a significant source for the ways in which they have represented schools and their local areas as well as the teachers, pupils, and employees of the local authority (Wright 2009).

Alongside this diversification of documentary sources, other kinds of historical evidence have also attracted the attention of historians of education. From the 1990s onwards, oral history has become recognized as a fruitful approach for the history of education. In the past decade, visual history has also become very popular especially as a means of discovering the everyday past of classrooms. Most recently, too, sensory history has begun to develop in this field of study as in historical studies more generally.

Oral history approaches in the history of education, seen as supplementary to and in some cases alternatives to documentary evidence, were strongly promoted during the 1990s by historians such as Philip Gardner and Peter Cunningham. Gardner stressed the significance of oral history as a means of understanding personal memories. As he argued, 'Within the archive of our own mind, the processes of remembering, commemorating, forgetting and reinterpreting ceaselessly operate to preserve what can be seen as a unique identity fundamentally ordered by narrative' (Gardner 2003, p. 177). In her presidential address to the Australian and New Zealand History of Education Society in 2007, Maxine Stephenson also pointed out that oral history could help to include a wide range of 'voices' in historical investigations, and went so far as to suggest that 'Developments in approach to oral history have transformed scholarship in the History of Education and have sharpened focus on the relationship between past and present' (Stephenson 2008, p. 3).

Visual history has been a further new direction in terms of methodology, in which photographs, portraits, prints, cartoons, films and other visual evidence have been increasingly enlisted to accompany and often challenge the established primacy of written texts. O'Donoghue and Potts, for instance, were clear that films, photos and architecture 'represent interwoven, sometimes conflicting cultural concerns and social relations that can enable the historian to explore the social and cultural influences that shape educational policy and life in schools' (O'Donoghue and Potts 2004, p. 477). They also made new demands of historical interpretation, but at the same generated fresh opportunities in that they could reveal encounters between teachers, parents and pupils and provide accounts of schools that, according to O'Donoghue and Potts, 'traditional histories of education often find hard to equal' (ibid., p. 478). Thus, Margolis and Rowe could examine what they called 'images of assimilation', photographs of Indian schools in Arizona (Margolis and Rowe 2004), while Burke and de Castro used school photographs to investigate the body of the schoolchild (Burke and de Castro 2007). Devlieger *et al.* (2008) have examined a large photographic archive held at Dr Guislain's Museum at Ghent for historical images of disability. For an earlier period, Richard Clay was able to interpret representations of the educationist, theologian and scientist Joseph Priestley in the many British prints depicting him during the French Revolution (Clay 2008). Films such as the documentaries *High School* and *High School II*, in the US, and the popular feminist film *Puberty Blues*, in Australia, could shed fresh light on the experience and challenges of comprehensive high schools (Rosario 2007; May 2008; see also Cohen 2003b).

Historical interest in the 'materiality' of schools and educational artifacts has also begun to be expressed in interesting ways. Lawn and Grosvenor, for example, have explored aspects of the history of material technologies in schools, which provide traces of the everyday past practices of teachers and pupils. These include low-key technologies such as pencils, slates, exercise books and ink bottles as well as larger machines including typewriters, spirit duplicators and photocopiers (Lawn and Grosvenor 2007). David Hamilton also notes the significance of school desks as educational artifacts, and demonstrates that patents provide documentary evidence of their historical development (Hamilton 2009).

'Sensory history' is an approach that has also developed more recently and although it has thus far figured relatively little in the history of education, there are promising indications that it has begun to attract interest. This involves foregrounding the non-cognitive dimensions of sensation, including the five senses of smell, sound, touch, taste and sight. Mark M. Smith has suggested that there is scope for a great deal of new historical research on the sensory worlds of children, and how they have understood the senses in the process of learning the social protocols and cultural expectations of their society (Smith 2007, p. 120). Peter Hoffer points out that this process has applied historically to adults as well as to children as they 'enter the sensate environment to conform to learned priorities of sensation' (Hoffer 2003, p. 6). For example, according to Hoffer, the receptivity of the senses, or the ability to describe what we have sensed, can be expanded with experience, so establishing a 'sensuous etiquette' in which the senses tell us where we belong in society and how we should behave in different circumstances and contexts (ibid., p. 20). This has significant implications not only for individual experiences of society but also for social and cultural relationships. Cowan and Steward, in exploring the sensory dimensions of the history of urban life, suggest that histories of noise, vision, manners, tactility, sexuality, gestation and olfaction 'show that sensuous encounters between individuals and environments are produced and structured, not just by their material features, but also by the particular social and cultural contexts in which encounters take place' (Cowan and Steward 2007, pp. 1–2; see also, for example, Cockayne 2007).

Conclusions

Overall, there has been a significant growth of interest in a broadening range of theoretical and methodological departures in the history of education in the early twenty-first century that raise questions around Herbst's critique of the field. This has taken place unevenly and often uncertainly, and the process still has a long way to go forward before it could be claimed to be universal. The tensions that have surrounded theoretical engagement are to some extent a continuing effect of the particular kind of history of education presented in the traditional historiography, but this is being addressed directly in some significant new work. Similarly, the methodological confines of much previous work in the history of education have been increasingly tested and undermined in a number of contributions to the field. Nevertheless, a key test of the extent to which such theoretical and methodological advances have influenced the field so far is to determine how far they have made a difference in substantive areas of study within the history of education. This is the focus of the next chapter.

7   The struggle for new directions

In the last chapter, evidence was found of new approaches to theory and methodology in the history of education that have potential to provide fresh intellectual vitality to the field. In the current chapter, I will take this further to investigate the extent to which these ideas and methods are being applied in substantive areas of study in the history of education, with particular reference to three key topics that have attracted much attention over the years. The first of these is social disadvantage and the exclusion and marginalization of specific social groups. The second is the theme of teaching and learning in the context of the classroom and in other educational settings. The third is that of education and Empire, with a particular focus on the British Empire. First of all, however, it is instructive to consider the tensions that helped to provide difficulties for an earlier initiative to enliven and reorient the field, in the form of curriculum history.

The case of curriculum history

Attempting to develop new directions in the history of education has often been limited in its effects because of the diverse constituencies of the field. Arguably, this was the case with curriculum history in the 1980s and 1990s. In England and the United States, the school curriculum provided a focus of activity that promised to help to reshape and reorient the study of the history of education more broadly. Significant work was produced in this area that deserves continued recognition, and much of my own early writing was based on this approach. If in the end it did not achieve all that was hoped for in terms of developing as a distinct line of research, this was due as much as anything else to the problematic relationship of the field in relation to education, history and the social sciences.

The history of the school curriculum began to attract broad attention in England in the 1970s in response to the complexities of curriculum reform and the insights of the 'new' sociology of knowledge. Curriculum initiatives launched with much fanfare in the 1960s had often proven disappointing in their results, and historical accounts suggested fresh ways of understanding the issues involved. David Layton's *Science for the People*, published in 1973, examined the origins of the English school science curriculum, and found that the political conflicts of the mid-nineteenth century offered clues to the eventual character and patterns of school science that had remained persistent to the present day. Thus, according to Layton, administrative decisions that were made in the 1850s for a number of social and political reasons 'set the seal on earlier events, and proved a crucial determinant of the place of science in the school curriculum' (Layton 1973, p. 160; see also McCulloch 1998a). Layton and Edgar Jenkins at the University of Leeds were very significant influences on my ideas as well as being very generous in allowing me to be the first named author in the joint book that resulted from a research project on the history of school science education since 1945 – *Technological Revolution?* – my first book in this field (McCulloch *et al.* 1985). This book investigated the tensions that had surrounded reform in school science and technology in England since the Second World War, and the frustrations that had attended successive initiatives. This was one of a number of contributions to the history of school science and technology to be produced in England in the late 1970s and 1980s, as the 'Great Debate' and then the Conservative government's early interventions in the school curriculum raised the academic and public profile of this area (for example, Marsden 1979; Waring 1979; Layton 1984).

Revisionist work in the history of education was a further stimulant to histories of the school curriculum. Previous historical accounts in the US and elsewhere had tended to celebrate the rise of an enlightened and liberal approach to the curriculum, and such works continued to be produced, but these came under challenge from interpretations that stressed the problematic social and political features of the curriculum (Franklin 2008). Examples of such new work in the US in the 1980s included Herbert Kliebard's *The Struggle for the American Curriculum* (Kliebard 1986), which examined competing interest groups in the development of the school curriculum in the first half of the twentieth century, and Barry Franklin's *Building the American Community* (Franklin 1986), which analysed curriculum thinking and practice over a similar period.

Developments in the sociology of education also helped to encourage historical approaches. The 'new' sociology of education stressed the ways in which social structures and attitudes bore a close correlation with the types of knowledge that were highly valued in the education system. In his classic work *Knowledge and Control*, published in 1971, Michael Young observed that

> We have had virtually no theoretical perspectives or research to suggest explanations of how curricula, which are no less social inventions than political parties or new towns, arise, persist and change, and what the social interests and values involved might be.
>
> (Young 1971b, p. 24)

His own brief historical investigation of school science concluded that contemporary problems in this area were outcomes of the social and historical construction of scientific knowledge (Young 1976). These ideas were developed further by another sociologist of education, Ivor Goodson, who traced the historical development of different subject areas in the school curriculum to highlight their social and political characteristics. Goodson's *School Subjects and Curriculum Change* (1982) demonstrated the preferential treatment accorded to academic subjects in relation to resources, staffing ratios, teachers' salaries and career prospects. School subjects, he concluded, represented substantial interest groups, each of them struggling for greater resources and academic status, and so a large amount of debate around the curriculum could be interpreted 'in terms of a conflict between subjects over status, resources, and territory' (Godson 1982, pp. 3–4).

Goodson's vision of the potential contribution of 'curriculum history' led him to establish a book series entitled 'Studies in Curriculum History' with Falmer Press, a rising force in academic publishing in the 1980s under its managing director, Malcolm Clarkson. Under this initiative a number of book contracts were offered to and eagerly accepted by a number of aspiring new authors including myself (McCulloch *et al.* 1985 and McCulloch 1989 were included in this series). In the flagship first volume in the series, edited by Goodson himself on the theme of *Social Histories of the Secondary Curriculum: Subjects for Study* (Goodson 1985a), he pointed out the need to develop further a 'sense of history' about the curriculum. He complained that neither sociologists nor historians had provided substantial historical accounts that explained the continuing dilemmas of the curriculum, and insisted that historical studies could 'elucidate the changing human process behind the definition and promotion of school subjects' (Goodson 1985b, p. 6). However, according to Goodson, curriculum history was 'less interested in history for its own sake, much more with history for the sake of curriculum – to aid understanding of fundamental curriculum issues', and he argued that this objective should stand as the 'litmus test' for those undertaking such history (Goodson 1988, p. 53).

This project effectively established the framework of further debate around the history of the school curriculum over the following decade. Nevertheless, doubts soon surfaced over whether curriculum history would succeed in establishing itself as a discrete field of study in the way that was envisaged. For example, Rob Walker observed a parallel between the curriculum disputes between and around school subjects that Goodson's research brought to the fore, and the aspirations of curriculum history itself to become recognized as an area of study: 'Just as rural studies found itself squeezed between biology and geography, so Goodson's study tramples on ground variously claimed by historians, sociologists and curriculum theorists' (Walker 1983, pp. 312–13). Similarly, Martin Lawn noted an emphasis on functionalist conflict theory and the notion of competitive groups searching for status, which he associated 'more with academics claiming research territories than teachers coping with work' (Lawn 1986, p. 227). It was doubtful whether curriculum history would be allowed to develop as a rival to more established and respectable approaches to educational, sociological, and historical study.

By the same token, skepticism was expressed over whether curriculum history had anything distinctive or original to contribute that would transform these already existing 'research territories'. In each of these areas, there was resistance to the expansive claims of curriculum history. Lawn's critique suggested that curriculum history was limited in its contribution to an understanding of curriculum change because it did not provide sufficient insight into the lived experiences and work of teachers (Lawn 1986, p. 226); dimensions that Goodson's later research was in fact to investigate in depth (for example, Goodson 2005, 2008). At the same time, there were historians of education who disliked curriculum history because it seemed to them to be too strongly sociological in its approach to be regarded as 'good' history. For example, W.B. Stephens, while allowing that Goodson's 'heart is in the right place' because 'he is a sociologist who is not antagonistic to history', remained of the view that 'unfortunately Goodson's appreciation of the nature and practice of history appears limited' (Stephens 1989, p. 451). Indeed, Stephens added, 'In seeking to persuade historians to allow their activities and priorities to be directed by those whose interests lie mainly in present educational issues, Goodson fails to understand the prime purpose of historical research: to recreate the past' (ibid., p. 452). For good measure, Stephens opined, 'Like the work of many sociologists, it is also littered with excessively long quotations from other secondary works, raising the suspicion that paraphrase and précis require too much effort' (ibid., pp. 453–54). Stephens was prepared to concede that some works of curriculum history were acceptable as history, but insisted that such work needed to be carried out by 'trained historians' rather than by sociologists.

These criticisms damaged the general project with which curriculum history was identified because they suggested that it could not easily influence different disciplines at the same time. Historians and sociologists would define it as being marginal to their own concerns, rather than as central to both history and sociology, while its aspirations to influence the nature of curriculum policy also appeared suspect to some. Another influential participant in this debate, William Reid, was more sympathetic to the value of curriculum history for an understanding of current policies, but warned that in order to achieve this it would need to be based on a particular view of history, concerned 'not only with past events but also with present action and potentialities for action' (Reid 1986, p. 81). Thus, according to Reid, 'Curriculum History will not be objective in the way that History has conventionally claimed to be: but surrendering that spurious objectivity it may become a truer guide to the understanding of curriculum change' (ibid., p. 82).

Overall, while the study of curriculum history produced a number of important pieces of work, it did not emerge fully as a discrete field of study, nor did it become strongly influential in different areas of research. The rationale for curriculum history had failed to penetrate the disciplinary boundaries of education, history and the social sciences, but had instead generated uncomfortable tensions over its nature and potential contribution, although it continued to develop and to offer new contributions in succeeding decades (see, for example, Franklin 1999, 2008).

The difficulties encountered by curriculum history in establishing itself over the longer term in relation to other fields of knowledge raise broader issues for other initiatives designed to promote new directions in and around the history of education. Such initiatives have often become frustrated by an apparent lack of responsiveness among other scholars. Moreover, they have tended to encourage some fragmentation or balkanization within the history of education itself, as sub-fields have emerged to represent a particular topic or approach. Thus, for example, June Purvis lamented that the history of education in Britain had been 'remarkably slow' to respond to the challenges posed by feminist history: 'While feminist researchers document and chart the history of women's education, their findings remain ghettoized and isolated from what is seen as the "main body" of work' (Purvis 1992, pp. 263–64). Grosvenor and Lawn have also suggested that

scholars with an interest in historical explanation move into or remain in discon-
nected sub-fields of study which encourage innovation; this has the consequent
effect of allowing the main field of study to remain secure in its approaches while
impairing its development.

(Grosvenor and Lawn 2001, p. 105)

It is important to be aware of such cautionary tales when appraising other attempts to
support new directions in the early twenty-first century.

Social disadvantage and exclusion

It is by no means novel for historians of education to be interested in patterns of social
disadvantage and the exclusion and marginalization of particular groups in society.
Nevertheless, over the past 30 years, and increasingly in the past decade, the conceptual and methodological approaches adopted by historians of education towards such
issues have been transformed. As we have observed in earlier chapters, in the 1960s
Marxist historians such as Simon in Britain and Katz in the US interpreted social
disadvantage and exclusion in terms of social class conflict. In this way they sought
to understand the historical failures of mass schooling and in particular the problems
that surrounded working-class education. More recently, this dominant approach has
been largely displaced by a wider set of concerns including gender, ethnicity and disability, and a greater awareness of their intersectionality. The attention given to social
class has been reduced over this time, both in relative and in substantive terms, and
the kinds of approach to social class itself have also shifted significantly. These new
developments in the field have at last begun to address key areas that had been largely
ignored by historians of education in previous decades. They have also been informed
by changing theoretical perspectives and by fresh evidence provided through recent
methodological advances.

In the 1980s, a new generation of women historians of education began in different countries to develop detailed interpretations of the history of education for girls
and women. In Britain, June Purvis came to the fore in highlighting the educational
struggles of working-class girls and women (Purvis 1980, 1989), while Carol Dyhouse
addressed the family relationships of girls growing up (Dyhouse 1981). In the US,
too, there was new interest in the history of education for girls and women (see, for
example, *History of Education Quarterly* 1984), while in Australia, Alison Mackinnon,
Marjorie Theobald and others also emerged to take the field forward in this area
(Mackinnon 1984; Theobald 1988). At the same time, and running in parallel, other
new writing began to document distinct lines of approach to the history of education
for boys and men, and the role of education in generating specific deals of masculinity
(for example, Mangan and Walvin 1987).

Histories of education for girls and women have both built on these earlier advances
and gained fresh insights from recent theoretical and methodological developments.
According to Margaret A. Nash, writing about the US,

As a field, the history of women's education has burgeoned in the last thirty
years. While historians continue to explore new arenas within the field, they

are also creating new theoretical frameworks for understanding those histories. Influenced by social, cultural, intellectual, political, and economic history, the field has grown richer.

(Nash 2008, p. 154)

Elsewhere, similar claims might be made. Biographical research has helped to reconstruct the experiences and lives of girls and women and to produce what Jane Martin calls 'a more inclusive education history sensitive to the operation of gender' (Martin 2007, p. 316). Martin analyses what she describes as 'the lived connections between personal and political worlds', arguing that: 'To map this terrain is to examine the ways in which individuals display self-knowledge through the creation and presentation of stories about the self across a range of social and cultural practices – both public and private' (Martin 2007, p. 521; see also Martin 2003). This is evident also, for example, in recent work by Kay Whitehead (2010) and Maria Tamboukou (2010). In Tamboukou's case, an analysis based on Hannah Arendt's conceptualization of biography within the political focuses on the life history of the US working-class artist May Stevens and the textual and visual narratives of her work. Other research has 'gendered the story' of the history of education more generally (Watts 2005), for example, by problematizing the gendered assumptions that have tended to confine women to the margins of science and other supposedly male domains (Watts 2007).

In the past few decades, also, new interest in the history of ethnic minorities and education has increasingly generated fresh insights engaging with theoretical and methodological issues. In some countries, including the US, this area of study was already well established by the 1990s; in others, such as Britain, it has been relatively slow to evolve. The literature in the US has tended to emphasize immigrant communities and also the problems of schools in mainly black localities (for example, Jones 2008, Olneck 2008). Recent work in this vein has explored the experiences of such communities and schools from their own points of view as far as possible. In Britain, Ian Grosvenor (2007) for example, has drawn attention to the uses of the 'visual archive' in approaching this history, especially in relation to black and ethnic minority children, while Kevin Myers has done much to reconstruct the previously obscure history of refugee schooling (Myers 1999, 2001).

Disability and disabled people have also found a higher profile in recent historical research related to education, again encouraged by a critical engagement with theoretical and methodological issues. Felicity Armstrong has noted changes in the social and intellectual context of this research that have facilitated 'the emergence of new approaches that recognize subjectivity, multiple levels of experience, the micro-politics of power, and the centrality of discourse in the study of social relationships' (Armstrong F. 2007, p. 553). Richard Altenbaugh has similarly argued that disability history offers 'a fresh approach, one that expands the scope and interpretive tools of special education in particular and social and educational history in general' (Altenbaugh 2006, p. 706). The ideas of the French philosopher Michel Foucault have helped to inform a range of recent work in this area such as Pieter Verstraete's study of the ways in which disabilities came to be problematized at the end of the eighteenth century (Verstraete 2009). A wide range of sources are examined to reconstruct the life and career of Ellen Pinsent in promoting the interests of those deemed to be 'feeble minded' in the early twentieth century (Brown 2005). John Oliphant has drawn attention to education for the blind, engaging with the technologies of literacy for the blind that were developed in the nineteenth century (Oliphant 2006), while Bernadette Baker has explored representations of deafness in the early modern period (Baker 2003).

While historical interest has thus shifted overall to these other forms of disadvantage and exclusion, the historical study of education and social class has also undergone significant reshaping. The previous emphasis in the historical and sociological literature of 30 or 40 years ago was on the working class and its struggles for freedom. Over the past two decades, this type of analysis has not simply been diverted into other forms of social inequality and difference, but has been directly challenged with the fall of the Soviet Union and the emergence of a new world order. At the same time as this broad shift in the political context, class analysis has also been affected by the social experiences of the past generation. The middle class has attracted increasing attention as its numbers and prominence have grown to become even more clearly a central factor in the development of society. The range of types of interest represented in the middle class, from the 'old' to the 'new' middle class, from the political idealism evidenced by some to the hard-nosed realism affected by others, also suggests a complexity and contestation that demand deeper investigation. The new literature on social class has moved forward from the monolithic view of the middle class that once was popular, to one that emphasizes a broad range, and to acknowledge that there is not just one middle class, or a single bourgeoisie; there are many (see also, for example, Power *et al.* 2003; McCulloch 2006). Victorian fiction such as Charles Dickens' *David Copperfield* (Dickens 1850/1948) can be drawn on to evoke the experiences of middle-class education in sub-standard provision and crumbling buildings, and the heights of aspirations involved as well as the brittle nature of its pretensions. Moreover, the published reports and evidence of nineteenth-century commissions often yield rich data for researchers on the everyday life of middle-class schooling (see, for example, McCulloch 2009b). Forms of social disadvantage and exclusion among the middle classes may appear less oppressive than those experienced by the working class, yet the social anxieties and fears with which the middle classes have been imbued give this diverse group some claim to be approached from this perspective.

The research that has developed on the working class and education over the past decade has often attempted to draw on the efforts by working people to write their own history. Jonathan Rose's magisterial work *The Intellectual Life of the British Working Classes* (Rose 2001) made extensive use of working-class autobiographies in this endeavour. Such an approach has also been pursued in the recent work of Tom Woodin on working-class writers, pointing in the direction of what Woodin terms 'more complex and nuanced accounts of class' (Woodin 2007, p. 496; see also, for instance, Woodin 2005). Complexity and nuance are also general features of the new historical literature on social disadvantage and exclusion that has emerged over the past decade, informed by a changing social and political context and engaging imaginatively with broad theoretical and methodological concerns.

Teaching and learning

The second broad theme that is useful to reassess in the light of recent developments is that of teaching and learning. Over the past 20 years, there has been increasing interest in the history of teachers and teaching, and this has drawn on a range of theoretical and methodological approaches (see also McCulloch 2004c). By comparison, the history of learners and learning has only begun latterly to shed new light on the experiences and processes of learning from the learners' points of view (a topic discussed in detail by McCulloch and Woodin 2010a).

Recent work on the history of teachers and teaching has moved on from the historical accounts that were familiar until the 1970s. These earlier studies were generally concerned with the gradual professionalization of teachers as reflected in the growth of their professional associations. In Britain, these included Asher Tropp's triumphalist portrayal of the rise and progress of the teaching profession since the nineteenth century (Tropp 1957), and Peter Gosden's survey of the contribution of teachers' associations to the evolution of school teaching as a professional occupation (Gosden 1972). Such approaches to the topic reflected and themselves informed the optimistic, liberal model of social progress that remained prominent at that time. More broadly, they also reinforced the dominant image of the expertise and beneficence of western professions that was especially widespread in the postwar period. These assumptions were undermined by a social and political backlash against the professions that demanded greater recognition for the rights of consumers and public accountability (see, for example, Perkin 1989; Halsey 1992; Freidson 2001). In the case of education in Britain, teachers came under sustained political attack, especially in the 1980s under Conservative governments led by Margaret Thatcher. In these circumstances, the somewhat complacent liberal histories were superseded by Marxist critiques of teachers and the labour process. This new historical literature emphasized the marginalized position of teachers, and their connections with the organized working class and trade unions (for example, Lawn 1996).

Over the past ten years, these class-oriented accounts seem themselves to have given way to a new wave of teacher history. This new literature consists of fine-grained, critical studies of teachers and their everyday relationships and pedagogies, based on a wide range of theories and methodologies. If the work of the immediate post-war decades stressed the long term project of professionalization, and the writings of the 1980s tended to focus on proletarianization, interest now turned towards understanding the nature of teachers' professionalism. That is, historians began to explore more deeply the daily interactions of teachers with pupils, colleagues and the public at large, and teachers' own experiences of their pedagogy and work.

Internationally, new research on the history of teachers and teaching also headed in this direction. In the United States, Larry Cuban led the way, in particular through his major historical study of classroom life and its underlying continuities and changes over the past century, *How Teachers Taught* (Cuban 1993). Linda Eisenmann indicated the potential uses of teacher professionalism as an analytical tool for the history of teachers, especially insofar as they could be informed by women's experiences as students, teachers, professors and administrators (Eisenmann 1991). Kate Rousmaniere produced a detailed historical investigation of teachers' work in the 1920s and 1930s, based on the oral testimonies of former teachers (Rousmaniere 1997). Professional identities and memories became key features of this new wave of research, and the experiences of teachers themselves came to the fore. The work of Miriam Ben-Peretz in Israel also reflected this trend. She interviewed 43 retired teachers in an attempt to reconstruct what she described as 'the history of practice over time' (Ben-Peretz 1995).

Further work in the British context developed these themes in detail. Wendy Robinson's historical study of teachers' attempts to learn through practice dealt with similar issues. According to Robinson, 'By seeking to clarify and define principles of teaching which rest on a clear understanding of the relationship between teaching and learning and the complexities of classroom interaction, this historical perspective can inform and enrich new departures' (Robinson 2004, p. 131). These concerns were also at the heart of a major study by Cunningham and Gardner, *Becoming Teachers* (Cunningham and Gardner 2004), which examines the historical development of the student teacher in the early decades of the twentieth century. This was a period when the notion of student teaching was vigorously debated and contested between competing interest groups. They focus in particular on the student teacher scheme begun in 1907, designed to provide intending teachers with an indication of the realities of everyday work in an elementary school, and to allow them a practical introduction to classroom teaching. In doing so, they make much use of contemporary written materials of different kinds, and also draw on the memories of retired former student teachers, interviewed for the study, to understand the experiences of student teachers from their own perspectives.

The nature of teachers' work has also been investigated through studies of the material realities of schools. Rousmaniere, for example, has reflected on what she has described as the 'Great Divide' between the classroom and the principal's office in the physical ordering of school space and the cultural ordering of the school day: 'As teachers are identified as adults standing by blackboards and athletic coaches as adults standing by their sports team, so too is the principal identified as the adult sitting at the desk in an enclosed and formal office' (Rousmaniere 2009, p. 18). Malcolm Vick also discusses the characteristics of teachers' work through an analysis of a set of photographs of Montessori methods at a school in Sydney, Australia, in the early twentieth century, and relates these to Butler's ideas about performativity and Foucault's concept of technologies of self (Vick 2009).

Other recent work has examined the changing cultural images associated with teachers and teaching, drawn from a wide range of sources. Weber and Mitchell have identified what they call a 'cumulative cultural text' of teachers, through which dominant images of teachers and teaching are transmitted from one generation to the next, but which is relatively unnoticed and unexamined (Weber and Mitchell 1995). Susan Ellsmore has explored representations of the teaching profession in films (Ellsmore 2005). Novels and plays also reveal underlying continuities and changes in such representations, for example from the life story of Mr Chipping in James Hilton's *Goodbye Mr Chips* (Hilton 1934) to the nostalgic regrets of Alan Bennett's *History Boys* (Bennett 2004; see also McCulloch 2009c). Christine Trimingham Jack (2009) assesses the working life of a woman teacher through the device of Lucy Maude Montgomery's children's novel *Anne of Avonlea* (Montgomery 1925/1994), the second in a series begun in 1908 by the better known *Anne of Green Gables* (Montgomery 1908).

Thus, the history of teachers and teaching has embarked on new directions over the past decade and more which are now well represented in the international literature. This is not the case to the same extent for the history of learners and learning, which has only recently begun to be explored in the same depth and detail.

A key growth area over the past two decades that has provided a starting point for an enhanced understanding of the history of learning is the history of literacy and reading, which has increasingly sought to illuminate the nature of readers and audiences and their interactions with texts. As Jonathan Rose has observed,

> Twenty years ago the historiography of reading scarcely existed. Many historians at that time doubted that we could ever recover anything so private, so evanescent as the inner experiences of ordinary readers in the past. Where were such experiences recorded? What sources could we possibly use?
>
> (Rose 2007, p. 596)

Yet, as Rose also points out, a number of significant works of this type have now been produced, deploying a range of interesting and unusual historical sources.

A further set of issues that should support the development of histories of learners and learning is raised by recent advances in learning theory. While the history of education has increasingly engaged with a range of social theories over the past 20 years, there has been much less interaction with learning theory including the classic work of such theorists as Lev Vygotsky, Howard Gardner and Jerome Bruner. Yet the implications of understandings about learning as a social process, for example, are potentially of high significance for historians of education. An interesting instance of this is the work of Lave and Wenger on situated learning, which makes an explicit call for further study of historical forms of social practice. Indeed, they argue, historicizing processes of learning 'gives the lie to ahistorical views of "internalisation" as a universal process', shifting attention to learning that involves the whole person rather than confining it to the cognitive domain (Lave and Wenger 1991, p. 51). Etienne Wenger's further work on communities of practice, which develops a social theory of learning, also pursues such an argument. According to Wenger, over time, collective learning results in communities of practice, which can be thought of as 'shared histories of learning' (Wenger 1998, p. 86; see also Illeris 2008 on other contemporary theories of learning).

A recent special issue of the journal *Oxford Review of Education* (McCulloch and Woodin 2010c) indicates some of the potential for cultivating the theme of learners and learning. For example, Elspeth Jajdelska, in discussing the learning experiences of eighteenth-century elite learners, draws on the testimonies of three individual learners to document the relationship between learning and social change in this historical context (Jajdelska 2010). Morag Styles investigates how *The Arabian Nights* helped to shape the thinking of future writers in the nineteenth century (Styles 2010). McCulloch and Woodin examine the dynamics of learning within the family unit in the case of the Simon family in the early twentieth century, and also some of the contradictions imposed by learning at a 'progressive' public school, Gresham's (McCulloch and Woodin 2010b). The learners' perspectives on radical schools are further elaborated by Catherine Burke and Mark Dudek in relation to Prestolee School in Lancashire, England, between 1919 and 1952 (Burke and Dudek 2010). Representations of learning in children's and young people's films are also assessed by Benita Blessing in the context of the former East Germany (Blessing 2010). This new work helps to demonstrate the nature of the social processes of learning over time, and also the interactions between teachers and learners in a range of educational contexts.

Education and Empire

Education often has both domestic and international implications, and not only separately, but as two sides of the same coin. Much research on education dwells on its characteristics as an aspect of domestic social policy, while there is a smaller body of work that highlights its significance as part of foreign and overseas policy, especially in the export of ideas and practices to other countries. Yet there is also another dimension to this that has attracted attention only recently, which is the relationship between the country's changing place in the world and the nature of education and society at home. This also relates more broadly still to an awareness of the interdependence of nations and the international and global nature of many challenges in the modern world. Globalization has latterly become an emerging theme in the history of education (see, for example, Myers *et al.* 2008), while authors such as Richard Aldrich have begun to develop historical perspectives on education and environmental challenges to human survival (Aldrich 2010).

Increasing attention has recently been given to the history of the British Empire and the nature of its contribution and legacy in the modern world (for example, Louis 1999; Ferguson 2003; Brendon 2007). Much of this general literature, such as the five-volume *Oxford History of the British Empire* (Louis 1999), has included little material specifically on education. At the same time, a substantial literature has also developed on the ways in which the ideas and practices of education in Britain influenced the character of education in different parts of the British Empire. This literature has generated interesting debates around the nature of cultural imperialism, the relationship between the 'centre' and the 'periphery' (see, for example, McCulloch and Lowe 2003), the extent to which imperial influences were beneficial, and the ways in which these influences were played out in different nations and areas. Latterly, there has been increasing interest in the kinds of resistance that developed on the part of colonized and indigenous groups.

Yet the educational relationships between Britain and her Empire did not run only in one direction. As Peter Burke has pointed out, there are evident dangers in a simple model of 'centre' and 'periphery' in which knowledge is diffused from Europe to other parts of the globe, in particular for the tendency of such an approach to take sufficient account of 'flows of knowledge from periphery to centre as well as in the opposite direction' (Burke 2000, p. 57). Over the last decade, there have developed the beginnings of historical interest in the reverse process, that is, how ideas and practices of education in different parts of the British Empire exerted influence in the imperial homeland. This new literature, stimulated in part by Edward Said's *Culture and Imperialism* (1994), has potential for a great deal of further development to investigate the dynamics of education in the British Empire which were rarely stable and often unpredictable in their nature and effects (see also McCulloch 2009a).

What J.A. Mangan described as the 'imperial diffusion' of British education (Mangan 1978, p. 110) around the British Empire from the nineteenth century onwards has become a familiar feature of educational historiography. More specifically, as Mangan's work, among many others, has demonstrated, English traditions were dominant in this process, and differed significantly from those of Scotland, Wales and Ireland (Mangan 1988). These latter traditions tended to be subordinated to the English while still retaining local support and potency (see, for example, Raftery *et al.* 2007). Mangan's own research emphasized the ways in which the great independent or 'public' schools of England established the ideals that were to become dominant in many different social and cultural contexts around the world, and also the active involvement of the products of these schools in proselytizing and implementing them in the British colonies (Mangan 1986). The universities were also to the fore in advancing the imperial theme, in particular Oxford with the strong encouragement of men such as Benjamin Jowitt, Master of Balliol from 1870 to 1893 (Symonds 1986). Other Oxford men who pursued the dream of cultivating the English tradition in the colonies were to include Sir Cyril Norwood, Master of St John's College from 1934 until 1946 (McCulloch 2007a). Yet it has also become clear that these powerful influences did not hold sway unchallenged. In a number of colonies, local conditions led to significant variations, adaptations and often active resistance to the imperial blueprint.

There has been much controversy over whether the influence of the British Empire has been malevolent or beneficial. Recent sympathizers have insisted that the Empire had a positive role in the making of the modern world (for example, Ferguson 2003). Such admiration is evident in some of the historical literature on the British Empire and education. Clive Whitehead in particular has defended the record of the British Empire, and rejected the idea that it was a means of exerting economic and political control over colonized peoples. Whitehead emphasizes both the idealism and the confusion of purpose that underlay British colonial policy, and insists that this did not amount to cultural imperialism designed to perpetuate cultural and political hegemony:

> Most colonial schooling certainly mirrored schooling in Britain, but there is ample evidence to suggest that this was more a reflection of local demand on the part of indigenous peoples themselves, than an indication of any deliberate British policy to colonise the indigenous intellect.
>
> (Whitehead 1988, p. 215)

Whitehead's more recent research on the British Indian and Colonial Education Service exemplifies this argument as he highlights the contributions of many men and women to building and maintaining public facilities and services in India, based as he argues on 'a genuine concern for the welfare of indigenous peoples' (Whitehead 2003, p. xiv).

It is also true that tensions developed in a number of colonial contexts over the character and effects of these imperial influences. In some parts of the Empire, these conflicts grew into open challenge and resistance on the part of colonial and indigenous groups seeking a greater measure of independence, or an assertion of national or local character. In relation to India, for example, the British mission schools according to Allender failed to recruit a clientele beyond their central city schools into the rural areas despite expansive programmes of evangelism and conversion in the mid-nineteenth century (Allender 2003, p. 273). They remained the preserve of the wealthy few, and had little impact on the general population. Instead, rival nationalist and religious movements took the initiative to extend their educational influence before the end of the nineteenth century (ibid., p. 288; see also Allender 2007). Allender's work indeed reflects the growth of activity on the history of education in India over the past decade which, as he recognizes, owes much to 'a more confident application of Western theorists in order to make sense of the colonial education experience in India' (Allender 2010, p. 283). Other British colonies have also attracted renewed historical attention. In colonial Fiji, for example, White has argued that the educational and 'native' policies of the colonial government helped to encourage uneven educational development and lower Fijian educational attainment (White 2003). Meanwhile, Swaziland in south-eastern Africa, a British protectorate after the Boer War at the start of the twentieth century, experienced tensions not only between the colonial power and the colonized, but also within those colonized populations (Zoller 2003).

Most recently, recognition has been given to the reverse processes by which the Empire has influenced education in Britain, which has until recently been somewhat scant. Edward Said's work considered the 'overlapping territories' and 'intertwined histories' of imperial culture (Said 1994, p. 1), examining how 'a post-imperial intellectual attitude might expand the overlapping community between metropolitan and formerly colonised societies' (ibid., p. 19). He went on to investigate how images of Empire have permeated Western culture, for example, in major works of fiction: 'Cultural texts imported the foreign into Europe in ways that very clearly bear the mark of the imperial enterprise, of explorers and ethnographers, geologists and geographers, merchants and soldiers' (ibid., p. 229). This key insight has underpinned a new historical literature focusing on the influence of Empire on the imperial homeland.

Early indications of this new interest have included interesting contributions by the historians Raphael Samuel and Linda Colley. Samuel's *Island Stories* (Samuel 1998) insists on the interplay of the imperial and the domestic, citing as an example the utopian strains of English life, reflected in the open-air movement and the rise of the Boy Scouts and the Girl Guides in the twentieth century, which were located originally in Britain's colonizing fortunes. Colley emphasizes the insecurity of Britain in relation to powerful neighbours and rivals as a key factor in its social and political development. According to Colley, 'Self-consciously small, increasingly rich, and confronted with European enemies that were often bigger and militarily more formidable than themselves, the British were frequently on edge, constantly fearful themselves of being invaded, necessarily alert and ready for a fight' (Colley 2002, p. 11). The consequence of this in Colley's view was that the Empire came to dominate Britain's culture and self-image (ibid., p. 326). Like Samuel, then, she regards Britain's domestic culture and politics and the growth and development of its Empire as being interlinked: 'The history of Britain and the histories of its various overseas ventures cannot be adequately approached separately. For good, and for ill, they were interlinked' (ibid., p. 305). Such points are open to debate. For instance, many historians and commentators have suggested that Britain's perceived security from invasion from overseas encouraged complacency and conservatism, rather than restlessness, in its social development (McCulloch 2007b). However, these arguments provide a point of departure for detailed historical research in a number of different areas.

The implications of this new historiographical trend for education have thus far been traced out only lightly and unevenly. John MacKenzie led the way in this area as early as the 1980s with his study of propaganda, public opinion and Empire and an important edited collection on imperialism and popular culture (MacKenzie 1986), and he has continued in this vein (see, for example, MacKenzie 1999a, 1999b). These contributions have highlighted how the Empire impressed itself on the British public through such media as the cinema, the popular press, consumer propaganda and popular literature. He singles out the Empire Exhibitions of the 1920s as exemplars of this kind of influence. The first, at Wembley in London, opened by King George V on St George's Day in 1924, attracted over 17 million visitors during the rest of 1924 and nearly 10 million the following year (MacKenzie 1999b, pp. 214–15). Its impact on popular awareness and construction of Empire is also vividly depicted in Andrea Levy's recent novel *Small Island* which recounts a visit to the Exhibition by the main narrator Queenie and her family: 'the whole world and only one day to see it' (Levy 2004, pp. 3–4). MacKenzie points out the significance of social class, the differences between the regional and urban centres of Britain, and the new immigration from the former Empire since the 1950s as factors in the reception of Empire in the twentieth century.

So far as the implications for and of education are concerned, some interesting and important earlier work was also produced, for example, by Castle and Heathorn on national identity and the elementary school curriculum (Castle 1993; Heathorn 2000). This has been taken much further by Catherine Hall, whose work has developed key connections between metropolitan culture and the imperial world. Hall and Rose have helped to explore a range of ways in which 'Britain's status as an imperial power became a part of the lived lives of Britons' (Hall and Rose 2006, p. 30). Hall has also pursued the issue of how the formal processes of education have helped to construct the colonial visions and expectations of the colonizers at home (Hall 2008). The powerful theme of 'Empires at home' has also been discussed in detail in a collection of work that grew out of an international symposium sponsored by the History of Education Society (UK) and held in Hamburg, Germany, in 2007 (Goodman *et al.* 2009). In this collection, for instance, Ruth Watts investigates imperial influences on British education in the nineteenth century, drawing on postcolonial theory and broader historical literature as well as comparisons with other imperial countries (Watts 2009).

We may therefore point to two general types of historical approach to the theme of Empire and education. The first, well rehearsed but by no means played out, has investigated the significance of empires for the development of education in its many colonies around the world. Education in the British Empire, for example, was based on a peculiarly English version of cultural imperialism but was often reinterpreted and challenged in a range of ways in different local, national and regional conditions. The second, developed more recently, pursues the impact of Empire on the colonizing nations themselves through the processes of education, both formal and informal, to demonstrate the interdependence and interconnectedness of social, political, and educational changes around the world.

Conclusions

It is important to recognize, as has been stressed already in this book, that the history of education has developed in different ways and at different trajectories and speeds in different countries around the world. Moreover, some of the new directions identified in this chapter have been potential more than actual in their significance for the field. The research that has been identified has been at the leading edge of the field, and there is a great deal of other work that would not at all be striving in new directions. Some of these fresh approaches might also be regarded as reformulations of established and familiar themes as opposed to being entirely novel. It should also be acknowledged that there are continuing deficiencies in some aspects of the theoretical and methodological engagement of the history of education as a field. Quantitative approaches, for example, seem to have become less prominent than they were in the heyday of Lawrence Stone in the1960s, although scholars such as Vincent Carpentier are addressing this area also (Carpentier 2008).

Despite such necessary notes of caution, the new directions taken in the history of education over the past decade suggest that Jurgen Herbst's criticisms of the field (Herbst 1999) were premature and would now be unduly harsh. Historians of education have responded to new intellectual challenges with vigour and there is much excitement evident at the ways in which the history of education can engage with theoretical and methodological developments in the broader humanities and social sciences. In the process, they have begun to address some of the most challenging issues that have faced the history of education. There is much evidence to support the claims of Reese and Rury in the US that a new and significant body of work is currently in development, informed by broader historical scholarship as well as by theoretical and methodological advances in the social sciences (Reese and Rury 2008b). In Britain, Goodman and Grosvenor have recently also found cause for optimism based in the intellectual and conceptual quality of new scholarship in the field (Goodman and Grosvenor 2009).

It may be that the key to sustaining the struggle for new directions such as this over the longer term lies in partnership and collaboration, not only between individual scholars but across intellectual domains and institutions. Curriculum history to some extent fell victim to territorial disputes and unresolved debates about the nature and contributions of education, history and the social sciences. Research in the substantive areas of social disadvantage and exclusion, teaching and learning, and education and Empire, provides examples of engagement with theoretical and methodological advances drawn from across this broad hinterland. Yet, if there are significant signs of promise and achievement in the history of education in intellectual terms, the strategic position of the field since the later decades of the twentieth century tells a somewhat different story, and it is to this that at length we must now turn.

8   The struggle for the future

This chapter appraises the changing position and health of the history of education as a field of study as it attempts to locate itself to survive and prosper in a rapidly shifting environment into the future. It does so first of all by discussing the strategic position of the field as it has developed in the late twentieth and early twenty-first centuries. It then examines the internal environment of the field, focusing on the organization and infrastructure of the history of education that has developed since the 1960s in relation to national and international societies and specialist journals. Finally, it investigates the external environment, in particular the relationship between the history of education and educational research.

Strategic visions

It is important to draw a key distinction between the intellectual health and vitality of the field and its strategic position. As has been suggested earlier, there is a good case for arguing that intellectually and conceptually the field is prospering. Yet the further development and even survival of the field depends also on its ability to find a coherent strategy within a sustainable set of structures. Campbell and Sherington (2002), from an Australian perspective, draw this distinction very sharply. On the one hand, they argue, there has been a 'great flowering' of the field:

> Old interpretative paradigms were rejected. Attempts to connect research in the discipline to the broader social sciences, and to establish productive relationships with mainstream history were often highly successful. Historians of education often had substantial things to say about the broader history of childhood and youth, the professions and of women and the family.
>
> (Campbell and Sherington 2002, p. 47)

On the other, they point out that the field is in decline in terms of its position in the curriculum of teacher education and in educational research more broadly (Campbell and Sherington 2002, p. 47). Thus, they argue, the main institutional base of the field is deteriorating and despite the vigour and achievement of its research its position is in grave danger.

In Britain, Lawn and Furlong have also observed a general decline in the position of the disciplines of education in general, including the psychology, philosophy and sociology as well as the history of education. They identify a demographic crisis that appears more acute within education departments than in the social sciences more generally, and worse still among those working explicitly in the disciplines of education (Lawn and Furlong 2009, p. 543). Moreover, they claim, in the educational disciplines in Britain at present, 'Critical mass appears to be replaced by micro-communities; common disciplinary work and accumulated insight seem either unknown or impossible; skill is replaced by willingness or audit and intellectual engagement with requisite publication' (ibid., p. 544). Indeed, they argue, 'The crucial role of a discipline in education in breaking down problems into its own logics and mediating between public information and problems, and public action is in danger of disappearing' (ibid., pp. 549–50).

In relation to the history of education, such concerns have been exacerbated in the case of England, as in some other countries, because it has been largely driven out of initial teacher education. As Richard Aldrich has shown, the history of education was formally included in the curriculum of the new day training colleges for teachers in the 1890s (Aldrich 1990). After the Second World War, its position appeared secure, and W.H. G. Armytage was not alone in celebrating its role in ensuring that a student could be

> made aware of the accumulated legacy of the physical, biological, philosophic and sociological legacy he is to inherit, and from which, through the personal transmission of gifted teachers (not all occupationally so classified) he will form his repertory of convictions.
>
> (Armytage 1953, p. 120)

Armytage's inaugural lecture as Professor of Education at the University of Sheffield in 1954 concluded that history should provide the medium through which intending teachers would obtain a 'synoptic vision' of the *speculum mentis* or map of knowledge (Armytage 1954/1980). In the 1960s, Brian Simon could declare with confidence that there was 'no need to make out a case for the study of the history of education as an essential aspect of the course offered to intending teachers', on the basis that it had 'long been accepted as such in most colleges and universities and is almost universally taught, in its own right, as part of the education course' (Simon B. 1966, p. 91).

Less than 20 years later, government policies in teacher education greatly undermined this longstanding role. In the early 1980s, history of education retained a significant position in teacher education, although concerns for the future were being widely expressed (see Lowe 1983). By the end of that decade, its role had deteriorated to the extent that it was virtually excluded from the teacher education curriculum along with other theoretical or intellectual approaches that were deemed not to be relevant to the acquisition of teaching skills and methods. Aldrich lamented in 1990 that a century after being introduced into the curriculum, 'history of education has been virtually eliminated from courses of initial teacher education, at least at the postgraduate level' (Aldrich 1990, p. 47). This gave rise to growing difficulties for the field in many institutions of higher education. As Wendy Robinson has observed, its 'professional niche' was at risk:

> The professional niche that historians of education once occupied is now an ambiguous and contested one. History of education as a subject of undergraduate study has largely been excluded from the world of teacher training which it traditionally inhabited. In the realm of postgraduate study, it has to vie with a restricted market obsessed with quality assurance, directly measurable outcomes and financial viability. Its ambivalent location, as it straddles the rival domains of history and education, has rendered it vulnerable to accusations of reduced status, worth and respectability within the academy.
>
> (Robinson 2000, p. 51)

As a result of this process, David Vincent, a leading social historian of literacy at the Open University in England, went so far as to complain that the history of education had 'almost collapsed as a subdiscipline, partly because those in charge of teacher education have driven history from the curriculum of training programmes'. Indeed, according to Vincent, 'Teachers entering the profession at the beginning of the twenty-first century probably know less about the past of their pedagogy than any cohort since formal training began two centuries ago' (Vincent 2003, pp. 419–20).

In the US, similar trends have been discerned. According to Robert A. Levin, educational foundations disciplines have been in '"retrenchment", if not retreat' since the 1980s (Levin 2000, p. 155). Levin observed that although in the early twentieth century history of education courses were required offerings in 'normal schools' training future teachers, such courses have largely disappeared: 'History has fallen victim to more methodologically-oriented programmes and to a declining faith in its purpose or educative potential' (ibid., p. 156). His estimate was that historians of education were present in only about 10 to 20 per cent of the 1,354 institutions that prepared teachers in the US (ibid., p. 157). At the same time, he noted that most of the schools of education in leading research universities included at least one recognized historian, and that as a group, 'we are strong and vibrant' (ibid., pp. 156–57).

In some other countries where the history of education has continued to be prominent in initial teacher education there have also been challenges for the field to overcome. In South Africa, for example, although the history of education survived within initial teacher education, it did not develop an independent scholarly society or journal (Randall 1987). In Japan, meanwhile, the history of education was included as a required subject in the teacher training curriculum under the Normal School Act of 1886, and although it was made optional under the Teacher Certification Act of 1949 it has maintained a position in the curriculum. Towards the end of the century, taking advantage of a broad public interest in education and a teacher training programme that was 'theoretically well funded', it could be claimed that the study of the history of education in Japan was 'booming' (Katagiri 1994, p. 639). At the same time, according to Toshiko Ito, 'In real life, a considerable number of educational historians do not only research the history of education, but also teach the history of education to students, who are frequently teacher candidates and occasionally in-service teachers'

(Ito 2010, p. 43). It appears that as a result of this the history of education in Japan became too dependent on its role in teacher education and the needs of the teaching profession, as opposed to the academic purposes of research, leading to fresh arguments about the future of the field (Ito 2010).

Thus, part of the struggle for the history of education has involved seeking a stable and suitable location, during a period when government policies and pressures within higher education have made university education departments and teacher training colleges increasingly vulnerable to criticism. In some countries such as England, this has led the history of education to become more rigorous and research-oriented while becoming less secure. In others, where the connection with initial teacher education has been maintained, the practical and functional emphasis on the progress of schools and the teaching profession has tended to continue.

The internal environment

The history of education as a field has sustained itself partly through the development of an internal environment that supports a distinct and discrete community of scholars and practitioners with its own infrastructure, debates and dynamics. This has become institutionally well organized and indeed strengthened over the past 50 years in many nations and also internationally. Let us look first then at the internal features of the field before examining aspects of its external environment.

The history of education has been organized in many countries, although by no means all, through national societies of members specializing or interested in this area. This has created an infrastructure for its development, and has generated not only conferences and other events but also journals and more informal networks that have provided collegial support and stimulated new developments. More broadly, too, an international structure has become institutionalized through the growth of the International Standing Conference for the History of Education (ISCHE). These organizations have brought undoubted benefits in terms of supporting a community with shared interests and values. They provide a home base and territory for the history of education, an institutional memory of its development, and a means of nurturing fresh approaches and new recruits. At the same time, there are risks involved such as being too focused on a particular approach or dependent on one group, or the possibility of becoming detached and isolated from broader interests and potential allies.

In the US, an organized group of historians of education first developed after the Second World War, when a History of Education Section, led by R. Freeman Butts of the Teachers College at Columbia University, was established within the National Society of College Teachers of Education (NSCTE) (Hiner 1990, p. 138). A *History of Education Journal* was launched at the same time, under the editorship of Claude Eggertsen. By the end of the 1950s, with scholarship in the history of education coming under increasing scrutiny from Bernard Bailyn and others, the NSCTE History of Education Section became an independent History of Education Society. Lawrence Cremin, the Society's first president, and Claude Eggertsen, its first secretary, arranged for the relaunch of the journal under a new title, the *History of*

Education Quarterly, which began in 1961. Yet one of the Society's later presidents, N. Ray Hiner, in surveying these developments, was still obliged to concede that this group remained both 'marginal' and 'vulnerable'. Most members of the History of Education Society were based in schools of education, but as Hiner recognized courses in the history of education and other foundations courses were disappearing from the teacher education programmes in a number of institutions (ibid., p. 142). According to Hiner, in this situation the most fruitful way forward was to support and cooperate with other groups and to promote the continued improvement of scholarship in the history of education (ibid., p. 144). Further to this, he warned, improved scholarship would depend on a sustained redefinition and renewal of the history of education itself (ibid., p. 146).

In Australia, a history of education section was first established in 1965 under the auspices of the Australian and New Zealand Association for the Advancement of Science (ANZAAS), but eventually in 1970 a new society was founded at a meeting held in Sydney (McMahon 1995, p. 1). At first restricted to Australia, it was extended in 1971 to include New Zealand under the title of the Australian and New Zealand History of Education Society (ANZHES). William Connell of the University of Sydney was elected as the first president of the new Society, with Cliff Turney, also of the University of Sydney, its first secretary. Here too historians of education tended to be 'isolated' and 'marginalized', but the new Society provided a means of providing resources in the subject for courses for large numbers of student teachers. The *ANZHES Journal* was created to begin from 1972 under Bob Bessant of La Trobe University who was its first editor, and was retitled in 1983 the *History of Education Review*. The Society provided an informal network of support for colleagues and students from many different institutions (ibid., p. 9). It gave, as even the gloomy assessment of the field by Campbell and Sherington acknowledged in 2002, 'an essential focus for the remaining academics, postgraduate students and others in the field' (Campbell and Sherington 2002, pp. 57–58).

I joined ANZHES when I took up my post at the University of Auckland in New Zealand towards the end of 1983. It undoubtedly provided a broader network than was offered within New Zealand on its own, where historians of education were few and far between (Openshaw 1987, p. 1). ANZHES conferences attracted substantial numbers at that time, and also supported critical debate and international fellowship which were also reflected in the Journal. Before leaving New Zealand I was able to organize an annual conference of ANZHES in Auckland in 1990 on the theme of 'Culture, politics and the history of education'. These activities were also well aligned with the more general infrastructure of educational research in New Zealand, and I was elected as the secretary of the New Zealand Association for Research in Education (NZARE). My monograph *Education in the Forming of New Zealand Society* (McCulloch 1986a) was indeed produced under the auspices of the NZARE and was the first in what was to become a successful series of monographs by different authors from a number of specialisms. I was also appointed as joint editor of the *New Zealand Journal of Educational Studies* which was receptive to historical contributions.

In Britain, a History of Education Society (HES) was formed in December 1967 at a conference held at the City of Liverpool C.F. Mott College of Education, attended by 150 participants who were mainly teachers of the subject in colleges and departments of education. The leading British historians of education of the time, Professors Harry Armytage (University of Sheffield) and Brian Simon (University of Leicester) lent their authority to the initiative by opening the conference. They referred in this to 'the growing interest in the history of education, particularly since the establishment of the Bachelor of Education degree' (History of Education Society 1968, p. 2). They also suggested possible new approaches to the subject, which Professor Kenneth Charlton, then of the University of Birmingham, pursued further in a subsequent address to this conference. The remainder of the conference was devoted to a discussion of current syllabuses in colleges and departments of education, and with a lecture on the relationship between Church and State (ibid.). The formal aims of the Society, which aimed to cover the United Kingdom as a whole, were declared as being to further the study of the history of education, to provide opportunities for discussion among those engaged in its study and teaching, to organize conferences and meetings, and to publish a bulletin (see McCulloch 2007c).

Thus, the British HES, like those developed in the US and Australia, was rooted in new developments in teaching, at least as much as it was in research. It was similarly associated with the concerns of educationalists who were based in university education departments and colleges of education, more clearly than it was with those of historians in university history departments. Nevertheless, early leaders of the Society such as Armytage, Charlton and Simon could engage with historians and educationalists alike (McCulloch 2007c, pp. 3–4). The Society's regular newsletter, or 'bulletin', attempted to draw these together from its launch in 1968. Moreover, the Society's new journal, entitled simply *History of Education*, set out to articulate a broader research mission. The first issue of the journal, published in 1972, included an essay by the leading social historian Asa Briggs, who defined the history of education as being 'part of the wider study of the history of society, social history broadly interpreted with the politics, the economics and, it is necessary to add, the religion put in' (Briggs 1972, p. 5).

My own association with the British HES began almost a decade later, in the freezing winter of 1981–82. I was working at the University of Leeds at the time on a research project led by Edgar Jenkins on the history of Leeds Central Higher Grade School, and was attracted to the theme of that year's conference: Educating the Victorian middle class (see Searby 1982). Some of the sociology research students of my acquaintance of the University of Leeds were not impressed as they could not see the purpose of what seemed to them a narrow and irrelevant topic. Yet I came down to London on a cold, snowy weekend in December and was struck not only by the quality of contributions but also by the warmth of the fellowship that the Society offered. I also discussed at this meeting what was to be my first hesitant venture, a short piece on the historian Martin Wiener, science education, and the historiography of national decline which was then much in vogue. The then editor of the Society's *Bulletin*, Peter Cunningham, was enthusiastic, and the paper was published the following year (McCulloch 1982). Over the years the *Bulletin* (renamed the *History of Education Researcher* in 2003) has published the early work of many who went on subsequently to become active members of the field (Spencer 2007).

The international field of the history of education was also to be enhanced greatly through the emergence and spread of ISCHE, which was established in 1979. This new organization also apparently owed much to developments in Britain, as an all-European seminar on the history of education was held in Oxford in 1978 and set up a steering committee (Tveit 1990). ISCHE was formally founded at an international conference on the history of teacher education held in Leuven, Belgium, in September 1979, and Brian Simon was elected as its first president (Luth 2000). Initially, it was based mainly in Europe, but slowly other nations in other parts of the world began to take part in its proceedings. This was significant partly in order to stimulate international advances in scholarship, but also as a means of discussing common challenges to the general position of the field. Jurgen Herbst, its president from 1988, regarded ISCHE as 'a meeting ground for colleagues from all over the world' (Herbst 1990, p. 86). However, Herbst was also conscious of international tensions between East and West in the final years of the Cold War, as, for example, he accused Karl-Heinz Gunther of East Germany of being 'a government agent instructed to pursue a political agenda', rather than an independent scholar (Herbst 2004, p. 339).

Richard Aldrich, president of ISCHE in the mid-1990s, pointed out the importance of increased international partnership at a time when many nations were witnessing a decline in the numbers of teachers and courses in the field, a trend that also led to a restricted market for its publications (Aldrich 1995). In this sense, the spread of ISCHE reflected the extension of attempts to develop greater collaboration in the face of a growing challenge to the future of the field, no less than of collegiality in research. A particular instance of such international cooperation was the publication in 1993 of an edited collection entitled *Why Should We Teach the History of Education?* (Salimova and Johanningmeier 1993). This was the outcome of a series of meetings of an ISCHE working group on the history of education as a field of research and as a teaching subject. The editors, one from Russia and the other based in the US, expressed in the Introduction their shared, albeit rather optimistic conviction that with the transforming international scene at the end of the Cold War, and the creation of a new world order, 'For the first time in human history we can ensure the fulfillment of man's most cherished dream to live in peace and friendship' (Salimova and Johanningmeier 1993, p. 6). This in turn, they argued, would require particular values to be encouraged in schools and teacher training, to which an understanding of the history of education could contribute: 'History of Education is one of the teaching subjects which can educate future teachers in the feeling of friendship, mutual understanding and deep respect for all the nationalities in the world' (Salimova and Johanningmeier 1993, p. 6). Contributors to the collection included six from the US (Hiner, Hinitz, Johanningmeier, Lascarides, Saslaw and Smith), three from Japan (Katagiri, Nakauchi and Seki), two from Russia (Rogacheva and Salimova), two from the UK (Aldrich and Simon), two from Denmark (Kruchov and Norgaard), and one each from France (Compere), Belgium (Depaepe), India (Ghosh), Norway (Gundem), Switzerland (Hager), Canada Mazurek), Poland (Majorek), and Spain (Sola). The collection itself provided advice on the subject and content of the history of education, the objectives of the field in teacher training, and programmes developed in different countries. A similar initiative led to the publication of an international guide for research in the history of education (Caspard 1995), and later an international handbook on the history of education that provided general accounts of the history of education in 18 different countries (Salimova and Dodde 2000).

In terms of supporting international research in the field, specialist journals in the history of education nurtured by ISCHE and the national history of education societies soon became very successful. The journal *Paedagogica Historica* had been established in 1961 with Professor R.L. Plancke as its Editor, based at the University of Ghent in Belgium and with a broad international range to its contributions. These were in several languages – slightly more than half in English, but many others in German and French, a few in Dutch, Italian and Spanish, and even one written in Latin (Depaepe and Simon 1996, p. 425). It was concerned mainly with the history of education in Europe, although it extended its range in later years and even from the beginning saw itself as 'the forum where historians of education in the various regions of the world will be able to publish the results of their researches and to discuss with each other their common problems' (*Paedagogica Historica* 1961, p. 4). This development, it hoped, would allow it over time 'to be able to establish the first basis of a general and comparative history of education and to contribute at the same time towards a better knowledge of the evolution of educational ideas and institutions in each country' (ibid.). In 1990, the journal was relaunched in a new series and with a fresh editorial board. It also published a supplementary series on a wide range of topics based on the themes selected for the annual meetings of ISCHE. The new series was much more adventurous in its approach to new developments than the old series had been, although Depaepe and Simon, two senior figures closely involved in its renewal, regarded it as a 'mirror' of the field more than as a 'lever' to promote further innovation (Depaepe and Simon 1996, p. 448). From 2003 it was published six times a year by Taylor and Francis, and its position was further consolidated by its inclusion in the Social Sciences Citation Index from 2006 (see also Depaepe and Simon 2005).

Another key journal in the field, *History of Education*, also prospered in the 1990s and in the early twenty-first century by appealing increasingly to an international audience. From its early beginnings in 1972, it became more firmly established when the publishers Taylor and Francis took over its publication in 1975, and it benefited from stable editorial regimes under first Kenneth Charlton and then Roy Lowe. I became Editor of the journal in 1996 at a time when its international outreach was becoming extensive. This internationalism was again encouraged by annual conferences, in this case under the auspices of the UK History of Education Society, which in many cases attracted at least as many delegates from overseas as from within the country itself. From the year 2000 *History of Education* was published six times a year, and by the time I stepped down from this editorial role at the end of 2003 its international coverage was a prominent feature of the journal's work (see also Goodman and Martin 2004). This international status was confirmed when it emulated *Paedagogica Historica* by being included in the Social Sciences Citation Index from 2010 onwards.

Undoubtedly the spread of such associations and specialist journals in the history of education provided the basis for communities of knowledge and practice to be maintained, and often to prosper. They supplied spaces for discussion, venues for debate, and outlets for new work to be published at a time when the field as a whole was on the defensive in many countries. The growing internationalization of the history of education facilitated greater awareness of the challenges that faced it over this time in different countries, together with mutual advice and discussion about the future.

At the same time, the consolidation of this infrastructure potentially raised issues about the isolation of the field and in particular its separation from the broader communities of education, history and the social sciences. Before the 1970s, historians of education had often published in general historical journals such as *Past and Present* (see, for example, Simon J. 1977) and also in generic educational journals like the *British Journal of Educational Studies*. With the development of specialist journals in the field, interventions in these broader forums became less frequent. As Goodman and Grosvenor have observed, historians of education have tended 'to publish predominantly in specialized journals and for a pre-determined audience' (Goodman and Grosvenor 2009, p. 616). The existence of specialist societies in the history of education could also lessen regular involvement in associations with a broader basis. In intellectual terms, the boundaries between the history of education and cognate disciplines became increasingly porous over this time. Strategically, however, the history of education was at risk of becoming more remote from the interests and concerns of other groups. This was at a time, moreover, when the external environment of the history of education was becoming steadily more difficult and hostile.

The external environment

As we have seen, the main body of history of education as an organized field of knowledge has been within university education departments. This has meant that research in the history of education has been closely associated with research in the broader territory of education. For many years after the Second World War, these were well aligned as the history of education was one of the so-called foundation disciplines that contributed to a pluralist conception of educational studies. Since the 1970s, however, the history of education has tended to become at least in some countries increasingly marginal to educational research.

Ellen Condliffe Lagemann, in her excellent history of educational research in the US, highlights the contested features of research in education over the course of the twentieth century (Lagemann 2000; see also Lagemann 1989). She argues that educational research failed to achieve internal coherence over this time, and that it was generally of low status both in higher education and among the public more generally. Indeed, she notes, 'Since the earliest days of university sponsorship, education research has been demeaned by scholars in other fields, ignored by practitioners, and alternatively spoofed and criticized by politicians, policy makers, and members of the public at large' (Lagemann 2000, p. 232). In the first half of the twentieth century, educational research was dominated by educational psychologists who sought to promote scientific rigour in the field through the development of testing and school surveys. In the 1950s, disciplinary approaches based on history, philosophy and sociology as well as psychology became influential as a means of enhancing the respectability of the field as a whole. By the 1980s, however, the need to provide 'recipes for practice' diminished the prospects for rigorous discipline-driven research (ibid., chapter 6).

In England in the 1950s and 1960s, educational studies offered a pluralist and eclectic approach to education that sought to apply a range of disciplines from the social sciences and humanities, rather than regarding education as a single and unitary discipline in its own right. As Richard Peters proposed in his inaugural lecture as professor of the philosophy of education at the Institute of Education, London, in 1963, 'education is not an autonomous discipline, but a field, like politics, where the disciplines of history, philosophy, psychology, and sociology have application' (Peters 1963/1980, p. 273). A grounding in the disciplines or in one particular discipline was seen as being essential as a means of understanding educational theories and practices. The key disciplines of education were generally viewed as being history, philosophy, sociology and philosophy, although others such as economics were also emphasized at different times. These disciplines themselves formed distinct and discrete comities, each with their own bases in research and teaching. Each of them involved specialization in their own mode of analysis, expected a particular kind of expertise and claimed their own unique inheritance of a tradition of knowledge and values. They were also dedicated to following the intellectual currents established by their 'parent' disciplines as they were practised across the university, often to the extent of being subordinated by them. At the same time, the disciplines were complementary to each other as approaches to the study of education. Combining their range of expertise was taken to provide the most effective means of addressing the problems and processes of education. Thus, the disciplines signified a pluralist vision of educational studies that sought to engage with a broad compass of human knowledge and experience. Together, they encouraged an approach to education that recognized its relationship to broader social, cultural, political and historical issues, of which it was perceived to be a part (see also McCulloch 2002, 2003).

The heyday of educational studies was in the period from the 1940s until the 1970s. In Britain, it rose to prominence after the Second World War and the Education Act of 1944, as part of a sustained attempt to reform education and improve society. From the 1970s it came under increasing challenge, especially after the 'Great Debate' launched by the Labour Prime Minister James Callaghan in 1976, and in the context of the educational reforms of the Conservative government in the 1980s. The *British Journal of Educational Studies*, established in 1952, reflected the key aims of the educational studies movement. On the one hand, it strove not to be 'narrowly specialist', but rather to 'serve the needs and interests of everyone concerned with education whom the implications of specialized research affect'. It defined its 'broad objects' as being 'to explain the significance of new thought, to provide philosophical discussion at a high level, and to deepen existing interest in the purposes and problems of current educational policy' (*British Journal of Educational Studies* 1952, p. 67). On the other hand, it offered specialized study rooted in the separate disciplines. In this receptive environment, the interdependence of the disciplines was celebrated in the 1960s in new courses such as curriculum studies and in publications such as J.W. Tibble's *The Study of Education* (Tibble 1966), while the distinct disciplinary communities also flourished with the founding of a number of societies and journals besides those in history.

In this way the history of education made a significant contribution to the study of education both in its own terms and in combination with the other disciplines. It helped to stimulate a pluralist approach to educational studies that drew opportunistically from the humanities and social sciences to seek to understand the changing problems of education (see also McCulloch 2002). This continued to some extent, as the Research Assessment Exercises conducted in Britain in 2001 and 2008 took care to recognize (Research Assessment Exercise 2008). However, from the 1970s onwards, education came under increasing pressure to be more accountable to current social and economic demands, leading to a growing emphasis on approaches that had a direct utility and relevance to schools and teachers. This general trend was witnessed in courses in education, for teacher training and continued professional development, and also in research.

At the same time, 'educational research' was promoted as a unitary and autonomous kind of study in its own right. In 1974, the British Educational Research Association (BERA) was founded as a major initiative to unite educationists around a common cause and a single organization. As Edgar Stones, one of the founders of BERA, later recalled, people with similar interests from different disciplines came together for the first time: 'It was this coming together of people from varied disciplinary backgrounds in informal stimulating discussion that provided the context and the impetus for the birth of BERA' (Stones 1985, p. 86). Its flagship journal, the *British Educational Research Journal (BERJ)*, founded in the same year, also pursued the goal of forging a single body of knowledge to supplant the disparate traditions of the educational disciplines.

Some historians of education already understood that they faced difficult challenges in this changing environment. For example, B.J. Elliott of the University of Stirling observed as early as 1977 that

> Among non-historians in University Education Departments and Colleges of Education, the study of Educational History has, for a long time, been widely regarded as being of minor importance and of little relevance to the needs of beginning teachers faced with shortages of resources, rebellious pupils and a cynical public.
>
> (Elliott 1977, p. 16)

Furthermore, according to Elliott,

> The historian of education traditionally therefore has stood uneasily between the worlds of educational social scientists and 'academic' historians, rejected by both and even now in the age of the 'New History of Education', misunderstood and judged by criteria largely inapplicable.
>
> (Elliott 1977, p. 16)

In this context, it fell to Brian Simon to attempt to find a rationale for the new educational research that would allow scope for fields such as the history of education to continue to develop. Simon was elected the fourth president of the fledgeling BERA, for the year 1977–78, and took the opportunity in his presidential address to address these broad strategic issues.

Simon's presidential address to BERA, entitled 'Educational research: which way?' (Simon 1978), emphasized the importance of BERA itself as marking 'a coming together from various disciplines [...] to create a new network concerned with educational research' (ibid., pp. 2–3). This, he proposed, should be concerned with the education of children across whole age groups, rather than with ways of differentiating between them through testing as had previously been the case. According to Simon, educational research should be based on '*recognition of the specificity of education as an object of investigation*' (ibid., p. 4; emphasis in original), which would entail submerging the undesirable aspects of contributory disciplines while 'extracting the most from them from the educational point of view' (ibid., p. 4). A 'liberal eclecticism' was not viable as a way of sharing problems common to the educational field. Rather, Simon insisted, resources should be pooled to seek greater understanding of the educational process, with the aim of enhancing the quality of life. Yet this was predicated on Simon's vision of educational research seeking out the broader structures within which education operated, functioning in an open-ended way to understand and improve the educational process rather than 'merely consolidating the educational system' (ibid., p. 7).

These lofty aspirations were realized all too rarely in the competing pressures of the decades that followed. The disciplines may well have been submerged, but they were drawn on only sparingly from the educational point of view. Moreover, Simon's own characteristically expansive ideals about education were rarely pursued in the face of demands to improve and reform the education system. A number of BERA presidential addresses continued to express ambitious hopes for realizing the potential of educational research. For example, Roger Murphy, marking the twenty-first birthday of BERA in 1995, argued that

> What is needed is high-quality educational research, addressing not just the quick-fire pragmatic concerns of hard-pressed policy-makers, but also building up a body of knowledge, insight and theory, steadily over a period of time, which will allow all those interested in education to understand its processes better.
>
> (Murphy 1996, p. 6)

This proved highly difficult in practice as a set of critiques of educational research itself emerged in the later 1990s (Hargreaves 1996; Hillage *et al.* 1998; Tooley 1998).

By 2003, as BERA reached 30 years of age, its new president, John Furlong, again argued for 'a diversity of approaches to research', which he saw as essential 'both for the different types of problem that need to be investigated and because diversity is essential for a pluralist culture' (Furlong 2004, pp. 352–53). Geoff Whitty, BERA president in 2005, concurred that educational research conceived narrowly would be limited as an evidence base for the teaching profession: 'Some research therefore needs to ask different sorts of questions, including why something works and, equally important, why it works in some contexts and not in others' (Whitty 2006, p. 162). Nevertheless, few historically-based papers were presented at BERA's annual conferences. Most of the texts in educational research methods, with a few notable exceptions, avoided discussion of historical method. Relatively few historical mono-graphs were published in education, while few funded research projects in education, especially of a large-scale nature, adopted historical methods or explored historical themes.

There were also occasions when educational research appeared explicitly unsym-pathetic to history. For example, Michael Bassey's presidential address to BERA in 1991 referred to three alternative ways of 'creating education': by playing hunches, through recourse to history or through research. He contended that the 'historical way' entailed 'repeating what has been done before: basing today's action on the way it was done last week or last year' (Bassey 1992, p. 3). By contrast, he argued, basing new developments on research involved 'asking questions and searching for evidence [...] creating education by asking about intentions, by determining their worth, by appraising resources, by identifying alternative strategies, and by monitoring and eval-uating outcomes' (ibid.). This kind of distinction serves to undermine the potential contribution of historical research in this area, and also the many contributions made by historians of education to the development of education in the past. Historians of education for their part need to make clear to their colleagues in other areas of edu-cational research that the work is also about asking questions, searching for evicence, and monitoring and evaluating outcomes, and that it provides an especially helpful strategy for doing so.

To some extent the history of education has also become relatively marginal to the concerns of educational research in the US, although Section F of the American Edu-cational Research Association continued to provide a base for educational history and historiography over this time. Network 17 of the European Educational Research Association also provided scope for historians of education to pursue contributions to educational research. In general, however, educational research too often provided too little encouragement for the history of education as an environment within which to grow, or to adapt.

Conclusions

In spite of the strong development of the history of education as a field of research, therefore, by the end of the twentieth century and in the early years of the twenty-first its strategic position in many countries was weak. Its position in the teacher educa-tion curriculum had either been lost or was subject to changes in government policy, and it was increasingly marginal to educational research. The internal environment of the history of education was structured and supportive as it developed new societies and journals that allowed it to maintain its position as an entrenched community of knowledge. Externally, it was in difficult and often hostile terrain, and its struggle for the future was far from won.

In spite of this, the argument put forward by Lawn and Furlong (2009) seems in some respects exaggerated. In the case of the history of education, it is not evi-dent that 'the remnants of the past live on only in the routines of method, not in the analytical strength of disciplines' (ibid., p. 549). Nor is it altogether clear that, as they suggest, 'The internationalization of fields of study and the growth of cross border study creates hybrids of different disciplinary histories and their production, or micro-studies which avoid the problems of the past while looking to the future and action' (ibid., p. 550). Analytical strength seems in some cases to be on the increase, and internationalization has often reinforced the field of study concerned. The history of education itself is neither a 'ghost' nor a 'shadow', nor something in between; and yet it is struggling to survive and prosper in a changing world.

9   Conclusion

The struggle for the history of education

The study of the history of education has changed greatly over the past century. Once a byword for dry, rather complacent texts about the progress of national systems of education, it has become much more diverse and increasingly stimulated by debates and insights drawn from both history and the social sciences. During this long-term process, the field has experienced and withstood many vicissitudes. At times it has been popular and fashionable, and the subject of widespread interest. This was the case in the 1960s for example, at least in England and the US. At other times its general image has been unfavourable. Rather than being central to education and history, it has sometimes appeared to be marginal to both.

Dwelling on the past record of the field, and lingering on its struggles, has thrown into relief many of the tensions and underlying problems in and around the history of education. Insecurities about its identity, rationale and future directions have rarely been far from the surface. These have been influenced by the position of the field in relation to education, history and the social sciences as the competing gravitational pull of each of these has tended to destabilize it. Yet if there is much in its history that might be criticized, the study of the history of education has also enjoyed many successes and achievements. It has benefited, too, from the commitment and tenacity of scholars and practitioners who have defended its cause even in the most unpromising of circumstances, and who continue to do so.

The history of education has been portrayed in these pages as essentially a contested site of knowledge, a condition rooted in its strategic yet unstable location in relation to history, education and the social sciences. Its contests have been played out in different ways in different countries and contexts. The geographical emphasis in this book, reflecting my own professional and personal experience, has been on England, New Zealand and the US. Other historical experiences in other countries have varied, although it seems to me they perhaps also share the basic dilemmas and issues involved, and it is important that these should be discussed and compared for further consideration in the future.

This book began by arguing that it would be possible to develop the history of education further by building on an enhanced sense of its past. While eschewing simple lessons, a number of themes have arisen from the review of its historical development that may be useful as a basis for discussion.

The first of these is that the struggle with the Whiggish, chronological model of social progress is far from over. This once dominant approach was undermined and discredited but was not destroyed. It lives on in many institutional histories of schools that celebrate the success of their own ancestors and predecessors, and often in general textbooks. It was a tradition that gave rise to works of impressive scholarship as well as to others of cloying sentimentality and some that died of boredom. It also provided a foundation for emerging education systems and for teachers, policy makers and other educators to draw on a selective tradition of progress. Yet its legacy has been damaging in terms of the reputation it left behind of an uncritical and basically unhistorical approach to the history of education, which remains a lingering rebuke to the field as a whole (see also, for example, Depaepe 2010).

The chief focus of the field is necessarily on education, yet as has been seen the definition of this has varied over the years. From being umbilically attached to the formal education system, it has found a much wider range of educational settings and contexts for exploration. Undoubtedly this is a trend that should be cultivated further, and this should also bring fresh insights to our historical understanding of schools and schooling in relation to these diverse manifestations of the genre.

It is arguable that the history of education has gained strength when it has articulated a strong and clear narrative or rationale. At different times it has promoted distinctive storylines that made sense of the history of education, in terms of social progress, social change, social equality or educational reform. These have been key themes for much of the past century. It may be that they represent seams for mining that are now to some extent exhausted, or at least require new sites for excavation. The idea of social progress certainly seems to have had its day. Perhaps one might conclude that the field benefits from a key debate around a particular idea or theme to stimulate inquiry, hold an audience and attract broader attention. If this is the case, it might be argued that it is not sufficient for the history of education to be 'post-revisionist', at least if this suggests a flag of convenience for a wide range of types of study with no overarching rationale, but that a fresh way of comprehending and explaining the past in a broad way is now overdue. It is possible that such a cohesive rationale could emerge from what Reese and Rury in the US discern as a new narrative frame of analysis that seeks to transcend earlier perspectives and represent 'a new maturity in the field, a willingness to embrace the complexity of education as a social and political process of change, entailing struggle but also growth and the hope of progress' (Reese and Rury 2008b, p. 7). However, this, although welcome in itself, may not suffice to advertise its general purpose or broaden its appeal.

It is possible to contend that the history of education is at its best when addressing aspects of struggle in the educational past. The nature of struggle can vary greatly, from overt and dramatic to tacit and disguised, from aggressive power plays to tactical and strategic manoeuvres. Yet a sense of the underlying struggles involved, and of the tectonic plates that move and challenge each other in the long history of educational change, seems a fundamental quality in the best and most enduring work. In the US, Ellen Lagemann has pointed out that the radical revisionism espoused by Michael Katz and others in the 1960s and 1970s was lively and important because of the passion and urgency that it displayed to study history and gain a vantage point on the present. She concludes from this that the history of education should maintain its relevance to contemporary social concerns in order to be 'more than a string of dates, facts, and vignettes' (Lagemann 2005, p. 17). Moreover, she adds, the history of education 'only becomes significant when it connects with enduring dilemmas or current puzzles and, in so doing, helps one to see the present in more depth' (ibid.). In England, the broad and lasting appeal of the work of Brian Simon might tell a similar tale.

In revitalizing the history of education there are also opportunities outside academia, for example in the interest regularly shown in history in the popular media. The visual media and the Internet are key forums for the public understanding of history in the twenty-first century, and the history of education embraces large themes such as the family, literacy and social inequality that might well be of broad interest in these contexts. I have argued before that the history of education can engage with an official past embodied in the agencies of the State and in the private past of individual memories, but that the forging of a public past that is debated and reflected upon in the public arena, through a wide range of channels of communication and media, may also be fertile territory (McCulloch 2000, pp. 14–15). This may also involve taking an active role in debates over the nature of history in schools and about the retention of records and artifacts. Historians of education have a potential role in helping to educate a broader public about the nature of education, and in providing independent and informed critiques that will challenge received orthodoxies and stimulate debate. Such opportunities also suggest a set of further challenges for historians of education themselves, to communicate through clear and straightforward language, to broaden their horizons to the public domain as a whole, and to make greater use of the new range of media and communications that have become available through the new technology.

New approaches in the history of education have often developed from changing concerns in history and the social sciences more broadly, sometimes by general consent and at other times in a delayed and partial fashion. It is vital for its health that it maintains porous boundaries between these cognate fields. Moreover, as this book has consistently argued, we should remember that there is not a simple binary line between history and education. The relations between these have always been complicated and complemented by the social sciences, and this continues to be the case. Yet if the history of education should be attuned to historical methods and social scientific insights, it should be no less alert to educational debates and be prepared to take part in these.

It is strategically crucial for the field to maintain the strong infrastructure that it has built in terms of societies and journals which have provided a basis for further development since before the 1960s. These have encouraged collaboration and mutual support. At the same time, they have promoted an increasingly comparative approach and an internationalization that challenges the insularity of researchers who find their comfort zone in the single empirical case. Yet it is also important not to retreat into the fortress of history of education, but to engage actively to influence the wider, external environment of higher education and public configurations of knowledge. Historically this external environment has been tended by university departments of education, although this has become less secure in some countries.

The history of education requires a substantial base for its scholarship and activities and must continue to search for a suitable place that it can call home. Just as it requires porous intellectual boundaries, it should also benefit from collaborative activity across the institutional boundaries of history, cultural studies and other curriculum fields of higher education. Once again drawing on the recent experience of the US, according to Robert A. Levin, despite the retrenchment of educational foundations disciplines in recent years a 'vibrant core of educational-history scholarship grows and thrives even so in the remaining educational foundations courses, in departments of History and Sociology, and in such programmes as American Studies and Women's Studies' (Levin 2000, p. 155). Interdisciplinary work with such fields as the history of psychology may also be fruitful (Gleason 1997), albeit that as Rury helpfully reminds us it remains important to be cognizant of the larger professional field to which historians of education belong (Rury 2006).

Although it suffers from underlying strategic concerns, the history of education also emerges from the account offered in this book as being interesting and important in its own right as a contribution to knowledge and understanding. It deserves broad support for its continuing endeavours: collegial support from within the academy and greater recognition from practitioners, policy makers and an interested public in general as to its ideals and aims.

Finally, we can return to the question raised in the Introduction about the identity of the history of education in relation to education, history and the social sciences. To what extent is it distinctive? I would argue that an awareness of the history of the field should help us to be more conscious and respectful of its diverse roots in different areas of knowledge. Nevertheless, it is not simply a pale reflection or imitation of any one of its constituent parts, but a broad coalition based on all of them; and it is weakened and undermined when it loses the contributions of one or more. The grand tradition of the history of education that reaches across the constituencies of history, education and the social sciences suggests a common and integrating mission, with a continuing potential to contribute to all of these aspects alike. There are many obstacles in the path to realizing such a vision. Yet it is this aspiration and potential, if anything, that makes the history of education distinctive and important, and surely worth the struggle.

Bibliography

Adamson, J.W. (1919) *A Short History of Education*, Cambridge University Press, Cambridge.

Adamson, J.W. (1930) *English Education 1789–1902*, Cambridge University Press, Cambridge.

Aldrich, R. (1990) 'History of education in initial teacher education in England and Wales', *History of Education Society Bulletin*, no 45, pp. 47–53.

Aldrich, R. (1995) 'National and international in the history of education', *History of Education Society Bulletin*, no 55, spring, pp. 7–10.

Aldrich, R. (1997/2006) 'The end of history and the beginning of education', in R. Aldrich, *Lessons from History of Education*, pp. 28–47.

Aldrich, R. (2000) 'A contested and changing terrain: history of education in the twenty-first century', in D. Crook and R. Aldrich (eds) *History of Education for the Twenty-First Century*, pp. 63–79.

Aldrich, R. (2002) *The Institute of Education 1902–2002: A Centenary History*, Institute of Education, London.

Aldrich, R. (2003) 'The three duties of the historian of education', *History of Education*, 32/2, pp. 133–43.

Aldrich, R. (2006) *Lessons from History of Education: The Selected Works of Richard Aldrich*, Routledge, London.

Aldrich, R. (2009) 'Obituary: Kenneth Charlton: 1925–2008', *History of Education*, 38/5, pp. 601–03.

Aldrich, R. (2010) 'Education for survival: an historical perspective', *History of Education*, 39/1, pp. 1–14.

Allender, T. (2003) 'Anglican evangelism in North India and the Punjabi missionary classroom: the failure to educate "the masses", 1860–77', *History of Education*, 32/3, pp. 273–88.

Allender, T. (2007) 'Surrendering a colonial domain: educating North India, 1854–90', *History of Education*, 36/1, pp. 45–63.

Allender, T. (2010) 'Understanding education and India: new turns in postcolonial scholarship', *History of Education*, 39/2, pp. 281–90.

Altenbaugh, R. (2006) 'Where are the disabled in the history of education? The impact of polio on sites of learning', *History of Education*, 35/6, pp. 705–30.

Anderson, R. (1983) *Schools and Universities in Victorian Scotland: Schools and Universities*, Clarendon Press, Oxford.

Anon [Simon, B.] (1953) 'Book notes: Educational pioneers "interpreted"', March-April, p. 11 (Simon papers, Institute of Education, University of London, SIM/1/70).

Apple, M. (1990) 'Ideology, equality and the New Right' (paper to New Zealand Association for Research in Education special interest seminar, Massey University), July.

Archer, M. (2007) 'The ontological status of subjectivity: the missing link between structure and agency', in C. Lawson, J. Latsis, N. Martins (eds) *Contributions to Social Ontology*, Routledge, London, pp. 17–31.

Aries, P. (1960) *Centuries of Childhood*, Penguin, London.

Arizpe, E. and Styles, M. (2004) '"Love to learn your book": children's experiences of text in the eighteenth century', *History of Education*, 33/3, pp. 337–52.

Armstrong, D. (2003) 'Historical voices: philosophical idealism and the methodology of "voice" in the history of education', *History of Education*, 32/2, pp. 201–17.

Armstrong, F. (2007) 'Disability, education and social change in England since 1960', *History of Education*, 36/2–3, pp. 551–68.

Armytage, W.H.G. (1953) 'The place of the history of education in training courses for teachers', *British Journal of Educational Studies*, 1/2, pp. 114–20.

Armytage, W.H.G. (1954/1980) 'The role of an education department in a modern university', in P. Gordon (ed.) *The Study of Education*, volume 1, Early and modern, Woburn Press, London, pp. 160–79.

Arnold, R. (1973) *A 'New' Educational History for New Zealand?* New Zealand Council for Educational Research, Wellington.

Ashby, E. (1958) *Technology and the Academics: An Essay on Universities and the Scientific Revolution*, Macmillan, London.

Bailey, C.E. (ed.) (1989) *The Imperial Background to New Zealand Education: British Traditions, Government Policies, Colonial Experience – 1400–1870*, A Documentary History of New Zealand Education, Part One, NZCER, Wellington.

Bailyn, B. (1960) *Education in the Forming of American Society*, New York, Norton Library.

Baker, B. (2003) 'Hear ye! Hear ye! Language, deaf education, and the governance of the child in historical perspective', in M. Bloch, K. Holmlund, I. Moqvist, T. Popkewitz (eds) *Governing Children, Families and Education: Restructuring the Welfare State*, Palgrave Macmillan, New York, pp. 287–312.

Baker, K. (1993) *The Turbulent Years: My Life in Politics*, Faber and Faber, London.

Balfour, G. (1903) *The Educational Systems of Great Britain and Ireland*, Clarendon Press, Oxford.

Banks, O. (1953) 'The concept and nature of the grammar school in relation to the development of secondary education since 1902' (unpublished PhD thesis, London School of Economics, University of London).

Banks, O. (1955) *Parity and Prestige in English Secondary Education: A Study in Educational Sociology*, Routledge and Kegan Paul, London.

Banks, O. (1968) *The Sociology of Education*, Batsford, London.

Banks, O. (1974) *Sociology and Education: Some Reflections on the Sociologist's Role*, inaugural lecture, University of Leicester, delivered 5 February 1974, Leicester University Press, Leicester.

Bassey, M. (1992) 'Creating education through research', *British Educational Research Journal*, 18/1, pp. 3–16.

Bell, D. (2004) 'Religion for a new age', *Times Educational Supplement*, 23 April.

Bennett, A. (2004) *The History Boys*, Faber and Faber, London.

Ben-Peretz, M. (1995) *Learning from Experience: Memory and the Teacher's Account of Teaching*, State University of New York Press, New York.

Blessing, B. (2010) 'Happily socialist ever after? East German children's films and the education of a fairy tale land', *Oxford Review of Education*, 36/2, pp. 233–48.

Board of Education (1926) *The Education of the Adolescent*, HMSO, London.

Board of Education (1938) *Report of the Consultative Committee on Secondary Education, with Special Reference to Grammar Schools and Technical High Schools*, (Spens report), HMSO, London.

Board of Education (1943) *Curriculum and Examinations in Secondary Schools* (Norwood report), HMSO, London.

Board of Education (1944) *Public Schools and the General Educational System* (Fleming report), HMSO, London.

Bowles, S. and Gintis, H. (1976) *Schooling in Capitalist America*, RKP, London.

Brehony, K. (2003) book review, *History of Education*, 32/4, p. 441.

Brendon, P. (2007) *The Decline and Fall of the British Empire*, Cape, London.

Briggs, A. (1972) 'The study of the history of education', *History of Education*, 1/1, pp. 5–22.

Briggs, A. and Burke, P. (2002) *A Social History of the Media: From Gutenberg to the Internet*, Polity, Cambridge.

British Journal of Educational Studies (1952) Notes and news, 1/1, p. 67.

Brown, A. (2005) 'Ellen Pinsent: including the "feebleminded" in Birmingham, 1900–1913', *History of Education*, 34/5, pp. 535–46.

Burke, C. and de Castro, H. (2007) 'The school photograph: portraiture and the art of assembling the body of the schoolchild', *History of Education*, 36/2, pp. 213–26.

Burke, C. and Dudek, M. (2010) 'Experiences of learning within a twentieth-century radical experiment in education: Prestolee School, 1919–52', *Oxford Review of Education*, 36/2, pp. 203–18.

Burke, P. (2000) *A Social History of Knowledge: From Gutenberg to Diderot*, Polity Press, Cambridge.

Burke, P. (2005) *History and Social Theory*, second edition, Polity Press, Cambridge.

Burstyn, J. (1977) 'Women's education in England during the nineteenth century: a review of the literature, 1970–76', *History of Education*, 6/1, pp. 11–19.

Bury, J.B. (1902/1956) 'The science of history', in F. Stern (ed.) *The Varieties of History*, pp. 209–23.

Butchers, A.G. (1929) *Young New Zealand*, Coulls Somerville Wilkie, Dunedin.

Butchers, A.G. (1930) *Education in New Zealand: An Historical Survey of Educational Progress amongst the Europeans and the Maoris since 1878*, Coulls Somerville Wilkie, Dunedin.

Butler, R.A. (1942) note of interview, 12 May (Board of Education papers, National Archives, ED/136/599).

Butterfield, H. (1931/1973) *The Whig Interpretation of History*, Pelican, London.

Campbell, C. and Sherington, G. (2002) 'The history of education: the possibilities of survival', *Change: Transformations in Education*, 5/1, pp. 46–64.

Cannadine, D. (1987) 'British history: past, present – and future?', *Past and Present*, 116, pp. 169–91.

Cannadine, D. (2008) *Making History Now and Then: Discoveries, Controversies and Explorations*, Palgrave Macmillan, London.

Carpentier, V. (2008) 'Quantitative sources for the history of education', *History of Education*, 37/5, pp. 701–20.

Caspard, P. (ed.) (1995) *International Guide for Research in the History of Education*, Peter Lang, Paris.

Castle, K. (1993) 'The imperial Indian: India in British history textbooks for schools 1890–1914', in J.A. Mangan (ed.) *The Imperial Curriculum*, pp. 22–39.

Chitty, C. (1989) *Towards a New Education System: The Victory of the New Right?* Falmer, London.

Clarke, F. (1939) 'Some notes on English educational institutions: in the light of "Planning for Freedom" in the coming collectivised regime', 21 August (Fred Clarke papers, Institute of Education, University of London, file 4).

Clarke, F. (1940a) *Education and Social Change: An English Interpretation*, Christian News-Letter Books no 3, Sheldon Books, London.

Clarke, F. (1940b) 'The English idea in education', lecture to Nottingham Education Society, 16 November (Fred Clarke papers, Institute of Education, University of London, file 30).

Clarke, F. (1943) *The Study of Education in England*, Oxford University Press, Oxford.

Clarke, F. (1944) 'Notes on the way', *Time and Tide*, February, pp. 172–73.

Clay, R. (2008) 'Riotous images: representations of Joseph Priestley in British prints during the French Revolution', *History of Education*, 37/4, pp. 585–603.

Cockayne, E. (2007) *Hubbub: Filth, Noise and Stench in England*, Yale University Press, London.

Cohen, D. and Rosenberg, B. (1977) 'Functions and fantasies: understanding schools in capitalist America', *History of Education Quarterly*, 17/2, pp. 113–37.

Cohen, S. (1973) 'New perspectives in the history of American education, 1960–70', *History of Education*, 2/1, pp. 79–96.

Cohen, S. (1976) 'The history of the history of American education, 1900–976: The uses of the past', *Harvard Educational Review*, 46, pp. 298–330.

Cohen, S. (1999) *Challenging Orthodoxies: Toward a New Cultural History of Education*, Peter Lang, New York.

Cohen, S. (2003a) 'An essay in the aid of writing history: fictions of historiography', *Studies in Philosophy and Education*, 23, pp. 317–32

Cohen, S. (2003b) 'An innocent eye: the "pictorial turn", film studies, and history', *History of Education Quarterly*, 43/2, pp. 250–61.

Cohen, S. and Depaepe, M. (1996) 'History of education in the postmodern era', *Paedagogica Historica*, 32, pp. 301–05.

Colley, L. (2002) *Captives: Britain, Empire and the World 1600–1850*, Jonathan Cape, London.

Commission on Education in New Zealand (1962) *Education in New Zealand*, New Zealand Government, Wellington.

Cowan, A. and Steward, J. (eds) (2007) *The City and the Senses: Urban Culture since 1800*, Ashgate, Aldershot.

Crace, J. (2008) 'Is inequality worse than ever?', *Education Guardian*, 26 August.

Cremin, L. (1965) *The Wonderful World of Ellwood Patterson Cubberley: An Essay on the Historiography of American Education*, Teachers College, Columbia University, New York.

Cremin, L. (1970) *American Education: The Colonial Experience 1607–1783*, Harper and Row, New York.

Cremin, L. (1980) *American Education: The National Experience 1783–1876*, Harper and Row, New York.

Cremin, L. (1988) *American Education: The Metropolitan Experience 1876–1980*, Harper and Row, New York.

Crook, D. and Aldrich, R. (2000a) 'Introduction', in D. Crook and R. Aldrich (eds) *History of Education for the Twenty-First Century*, pp. ix–xi.

Crook, D. and Aldrich, R. (eds) (2000b) *History of Education for the Twenty-First Century*, Institute of Education, London.

Crossman, R. (1979) *The Crossman Diaries: Selections from the Diaries of a Cabinet Minister 1964–1970*, introduced and edited by Anthony Howard, Magnum Books, London.

Cuban, L. (1993) *How Teachers Taught: Constancy and Change in American Classrooms, 1880–1980*, Teachers College Press, New York.

Cubberley, E.P. (1934) *Public Education in the United States: A Study and Interpretation of American Educational History*, revised and enlarged edition, Houghton Mifflin Company, Boston.

Cumming, I. (1959) *Glorious Enterprise: The History of the Auckland Education Board, 1857–1957*, Whitcombe and Tombs, Auckland.

Cumming, I. and Cumming, A. (1978) *History of State Education in New Zealand, 1840–1975*, Pitman, Wellington.

Cunningham, P. and Gardner, P. (2004) *Becoming Teachers: Texts and Testimonies 1907–1950*, Woburn Press, London.

Cunningham, P. and Martin, J. (eds) (2004) special issue, 'Brian Simon', *History of Education*, 33/5.

Curtis, S.J. (1948) *History of Education in Great Britain*, University Tutorial Press, London.

Daglish, N., McCulloch, G., Miller, P., Shuker, R. (1989) Forum: 'A "One Best System" in New Zealand', *History of Education Quarterly*, 29/2, pp. 261–77

Daily Mail (2008) report, 'The failed generation: A million teenagers lack basic skills after they were "let down by the Government"', 20 April.

Daily Telegraph (2007) report, 'David Cameron: Labour has failed a generation', 24 August.

Davey, I. (1987) 'Capitalism, patriarchy and the origins of mass schooling', *History of Education Review*, 16/2, pp. 1–12.

Davey, I. (1992) 'Capitalism, patriarchy and the origins of mass schooling: the radical debate', in A. Rattansi and D. Reeder (eds) (1992) *Rethinking Radical Education: Essays in Honour of Brian Simon*, Lawrence and Wishart, London, pp. 169–95.

Daybell, J. (2005) 'Interpreting letters and reading script: evidence for female education and literacy in Tudor England', *History of Education*, 34/6, pp. 695–715.

Denzin, N.K., Lincoln, Y.S., Smith, L.T. (eds) (2008) *Handbook of Critical and Indigenous Methodologies*, Sage, London.

Depaepe, M. (1993) 'History of education anno 1992: "A tale told by an idiot, full of sound and fury, signifying nothing"?', *History of Education*, 22/1, pp. 1–10.

Depaepe, M. (2003) 'What kind of history of education may we expect for the twenty-first century? Some comments on four recent readers in the field', *Paedagogica Historica*, 39/1–2, pp. 187–99.

Depaepe, M. (2007) 'Philosophy and history of education: time to bridge the gap?', *Educational Philosophy and History*, 39/1, pp. 28–43.

Depaepe, M. (2010) 'The ten commandments of good practices in history of education research', *Zeitschrift für Pädagogische Historiographie*, 16/1, pp. 31–34.

Depaepe, M. and Simon, F. (1996) '*Paedagogica Historica*: lever or mirror in the making of the history of education?', *Paedagogica Historica*, 32/2, pp. 421–50.

Depaepe, M. and Simon, F. (2005) '*Paedagogica Historica*: vehicule de l'internationalisation de l'histoire de l'education?', *Annali di storia dell' educazione e delle istituzioni scholastiche*, 12, pp. 345–61.

Department for Education (1992) *Choice and Diversity: A New Framework for Schools*, HMSO, London.

Department for Education (1997) *Excellence in Schools*, HMSO, London.

Department of Education and Science (1986) *A New Choice of School: City Technology Colleges*, HMSO, London.

Devlieger, P., Grosvenor, I., Simon, F., Van Hove, G., and Vanobbergen, B. (2008) 'Visualising disability in the past', *Paedagogica Historica*, 44/6, pp. 747–60.

Dickens, C. (1850/1948) *The Personal History of David Copperfield*, Oxford University Press, Oxford.

Donato, R. and Lazerson, M. (2000) 'New directions in American educational history: problems and prospects', *Educational Researcher*, 29/8, pp. 4–15.

Durkheim, E. (1956) *Education and Sociology*, Free Press, New York.

Durkheim, E. (1977) *The Evolution of Educational Thought: Lectures on the Formation and Development of Secondary Education in France*, RKP, London.

Dyhouse, C. (1981) *Girls Growing up in Late Victorian and Edwardian England*, Routledge, London.

Eccles, J.R. (1948) *My Life as a Public School Master*, The Times Printing Works, Blackburn.

Eisenmann, L. (1991) 'Teacher professionalism: a new analytical tool for the history of teachers', *Harvard Educational Review*, 61/2, pp. 215–24.

Elliott, B.J. (1977) 'Researching the history of education', *British Educational Research Journal*, 3/2, pp. 16–19.

Ellsmore, S. (2005) *Carry on, Teachers! Representations of the Teaching Profession in Screen Culture*, Stoke on Trent, Trentham.

Evans, R. (1997) *In Defence of History*, Granta Books, London.

Ewing, E. and Hicks, D. (eds) (2006) *Education and the Great Depression: Lessons from a Global History*, Peter Lang, New York.

Ferguson, N. (ed.) (1997) *Virtual History: Alternatives and Counterfactuals*, Picador, London.

Ferguson, N. (2003) *Empire: How Britain Made the Modern World*, Allen Lane, London.

Fitzgerald, T. (2005) 'Archives of memory and memories of archives: CMS women's letters and diaries 1823–35', *History of Education*, 34/6, pp. 657–74.

Franklin, B. (1986) *Building the American Curriculum: The School Curriculum and the Search for Social Control*, Falmer Press, London.

Franklin, B. (1999) 'The state of curriculum history', *History of Education*, 28/4, pp. 459–63.

Franklin, B. (2005) '"Gone before you know it": urban school reform and the short life of the Education Action Zone initiative', *London Review of Education*, 3/2, pp. 3–27.

Franklin, B. (2008) 'Curriculum history and its revisionist legacy', in W. Reese and J. Rury (eds) *Rethinking the History of American Education*, pp. 223–43.

Freidson, E. (2001) *Professionalism: The Third Logic*, Cambridge, Polity Press.

Furlong, J. (2004) 'BERA at 30. Have we come of age?', *British Educational Research Journal*, 30/3, pp. 343–58.

Gardner, P. (2003) 'Oral history in education: teacher's memory and teachers' history', *History of Education*, 32/2, pp. 175–88.

Gardner, P. (1996) 'Deciding to teach: the making of elementary school teachers in the early twentieth century', in M. Chase and I. Dyck (eds) *Living and Learning: Essays in Honour of J.F.C. Harrison*, Aldershot, Scholar Press, pp. 236–51.

Glass, D.V. (ed.) (1954) *Social Mobility in Britain*, Routledge, London.

Gleason, M. (1997) 'The history of psychology and the history of education: what can interdisciplinary research offer?', *Historical Studies in Education*, 9/1, pp. 98–106.

Goodman, J. (2003) 'Troubling histories and theories: gender and the history of education', *History of Education*, 32/2, pp. 157–74.

Goodman, J. and Grosvenor, I. (2009) 'Educational research – history of education a curious case?', *Oxford Review of Education*, 35/5, pp. 601–16.

Goodman, J., McCulloch, G., Richardson, W. (eds) (2008) *Social Change in the History of British Education*, Routledge, London.

Goodman, J., McCulloch, G., Richardson, W. (eds) (2009) special issue, '"Empires Overseas" and "Empires at Home": Postcolonial and transnational perspectives on social change in the history of education', *Paedagogica Historica*, 45/6.

Goodman, J. and Martin, J. (2004) 'Editorial: *History of Education* – defining the field', *History of Education*, 33/1, pp. 1–10.

Goodson, I. (1982) *School Subjects and Curriculum Change*, Croom Helm, London.

Goodson, I. (ed.) (1985a) *Social Histories of the Secondary Curriculum: Subjects for Study*, London, Falmer Press.

Goodson, I. (1985b) 'Towards curriculum history', in I. Goodson (ed.) *Social Histories of the Secondary Curriculum*, pp. 1–8.

Goodson, I. (1988) *The Making of Curriculum: Collected Essays*, Falmer, London.

Goodson, I. (2005) *Learning, Curriculum and Life Politics: The Selected Works of Ivor F. Goodson*, Routledge, London.

Goodson, I. (2008) *Investigating the Teacher's Life and Work*, Rotterdam, Sense.

Gordon, P. (ed.) (1980) *The Study of Education: A Collection of Inaugural Lectures*, volume 1, Early and Modern, Woburn Press, London.

Gordon, P. and Szreter, R. (1989a) 'Introduction', in P. Gordon and R. Szreter (eds) *History of Education*, pp. 1–18.

Gordon, P. and Szreter, R. (eds) (1989b) *History of Education: The Making of a Discipline*, Woburn, London.

Gosden, P. (1972) *The Evolution of a Profession: A Study of the Contribution of Teachers' Associations to the Development of School Teaching as a Professional Occupation*, Basil Blackwell, Oxford.

Gosden, P. (1984) 'National policy and the rehabilitation of the practical: the context', in D. Layton (ed.) *The Alternative Road: The Rehabilitation of the Practical*, University of Leeds, Leeds, pp. 7–20.

Gove, M. (2008) *A Failed Generation: Educational Inequality under Labour*, Conservative Party, London.

Grace, G. (1990) 'Notes on the schooling of the English working class: what lessons for New Zealand? A comparative briefing paper', in Hugh Lauder and Cathy Wylie (eds) *Towards Successful Schooling*, Falmer, London, pp. 105–19.

Grosvenor, I. (1997) *Assimilating Identities: Racism and Educational Policy in Post 1945 Britain*, Lawrence and Wishart, London.

Grosvenor, I. (2007) 'From the "eye of history" to a "second gaze": the visual archive and the marginalized in the history of education', *History of Education*, 36/4–5, pp. 607–22.

Grosvenor, I. and Lawn, M. (2001) 'Ways of seeing in education and schooling: emerging historiographies', *History of Education*, 30/2, pp. 105–08.

Hall, C. (2008) 'Making colonial subjects: education in the age of empire', *Paedagogica Historica*, 37/6, pp. 773–87.

Hall, C. and Rose, S. (2006) 'Introduction: Being at home with the Empire', in C. Hall, S. Rose (eds) *At Home with the Empire: Metropolitan Culture and the Imperial World*, Cambridge University Press, Cambridge, pp. 1–31.

Halsey, A.H. (1954) 'The relation between education and social mobility with particular reference to the grammar school since 1944' (unpublished PhD thesis, London School of Economics, University of London).

Halsey, A.H. (1992) *The Decline of Donnish Dominion: The British Academic Professions in the 20th Century*, Oxford, Clarendon Press.

Halsey, A.H., Heath, A., Ridge, J. (1980) *Origins and Destinations: Family, Class and Education in Modern Britain*, Clarendon Press, Oxford.

Hamilton, D. (2009) 'Patents: a neglected source in the history of education', *History of Education*, 38/2, pp. 303–10.

Handlin, O. (1961) 'Introductory note', *Harvard Educational Review*, 31/2, pp. 121–23.

Hansot, E. and Tyack, D. (1982) 'A usable past: using history in educational policy', in A. Lieberman, M.W. McLaughlin (eds) *Policy Making in Education*, National Society for Study of Education, Chicago, pp. 1–21.

Hargreaves, D. (1996) *Teaching as a Research-Based Profession: Possibilities and Prospects*, TTA Annual Lecture, London, Teacher Training Agency.

Hawthorn, G. (1991) *Plausible Worlds: Possibility and Understanding in History and the Social Sciences*, Cambridge University Press, Cambridge.

Heathorn, S. (2000) *For Home, Country, and Race: Constructing Gender, Class and Englishness in the Elementary School, 1800–1914*, University of Toronto Press, Toronto.

Herbst, J. (1980) 'Beyond the debate over revisionism: three educational pasts writ large', *History of Education Quarterly*, 20/2, pp. 131–45.

Herbst, J. (1990) 'The International Standing Conference for the History of Education after the first decade', *Paedagogica Historica*, 26/1, pp. 85–89.

Herbst, J. (1999) 'The history of education: state of the art at the turn of the century in Europe and North America', *Paedagogica Historica*, 35/3, pp. 737–47.

Herbst, J. (2004) Essay review: 'The Communist bourgeois as victim', *Paedagogica Historica*, 40/3, pp. 335–39.

Higginson, J.H. (1980) 'Establishing a history of education course: the work of Professor Michael Sadler, 1903–11', *History of Education*, 9/3, pp. 245–55.

Hillage, J., Pearson, R., Anderson, A., Tamkin, P. (1998) *Excellence in Research on Schools*, Department for Education and Employment, London.

Hilton, J. (1934) *Goodbye Mr Chips*, Hodder and Stoughton, London.

Hiner, N.R. (1990) 'History of education for the 1990s and beyond: the case for academic imperialism', *History of Education Quarterly*, 30/2, pp. 137–59.

History of Education Quarterly (1984), special issue, 'The history of education for girls and women', 24/1.

History of Education Society (1968) *Bulletin*, Editorial, p. 2.

Hoffer, P. (2003) *Sensory Worlds in Early America*, Johns Hopkins University Press, London.

Hoggart, R. (1958) *The Uses of Literacy: Aspects of Working-Class Life with Special Reference to Publications and Entertainments*, Chatto and Windus, London.

Humes, W. and Paterson, H. (eds) (1983) *Scottish Culture and Scottish Education*, J. Donald, Edinburgh.

Humphries, S. (1981) *Hooligans or Rebels? An Oral History of Working Class Childhood and Youth*, Blackwell, Oxford.

Illeris, K. (ed.) (2008) *Contemporary Theories of Learning*, Routledge, London.

Ito, T. (2010) 'Historians and the present: on Marc Depaepe's Decalogue', *Zeitschrift für Pädagogische Historiographie*, 16/1, pp. 43–45.

Jajdelska, E. (2010) '"The very defective and erroneous method": reading instruction and social identity in elite eighteenth-century learners', *Oxford Review of Education*, 36/2, pp. 141–56.

Johnson, R. (1970) 'Educational policy and social control in early Victorian England', *Past and Present*, 49, pp. 96–119.

Jones, B. (2004) 'Simon, Ernest Emil Darwin', in *Oxford Dictionary of National Biography*, volume 50, pp. 663–65.

Jones, J. (2008) 'All educational politics are local: new perspectives on black schooling in the postbellum South', in W. Reese and J. Rury (eds) *Rethinking the History of American Education*, pp. 47–71.

Judges, A.V. (ed.) (1952) *Pioneers of English Education*, Faber and Faber, London.

Karier, C.H. (1979) 'The quest for orderly change: some reflections', *History of Education Quarterly*, 19/2, pp. 159–77.

Katagiri, Y. (1994) 'The study of the history of education in Japan', *Paedagogica Historica*, 30/2, pp. 637–44.

Katz, M. (1968) *The Irony of Early School Reform: Educational Innovation in Mid-Nineteenth Century Massachusetts*, Harvard University Press, Cambridge, Mass.

Katz, M. (1987) *Reconstructing American Education*, Cambridge, Mass., Harvard University Press, Cambridge, Mass.

Kaye, H. (1984) *The British Marxist Historians: An Introductory Analysis*, Polity Press, Cambridge.

Kliebard, H. (1986) *The Struggle for the American Curriculum, 1893–1958*, Routledge and Kegan Paul, Boston.

Lagemann, E.C. (1989) 'The plural worlds of education research', *History of Education Quarterly*, 29, pp. 185–214.

Lagemann, E.C. (2000) *An Elusive Science: The Troubling History of Education Research*, University of Chicago Press, Chicago.

Lagemann, E.C. (2005) 'Does history matter in education research? A brief for the humanities in an age of science', *Harvard Educational Review*, 75/1, pp. 9–24.

Lave, J. and Wenger, E. (1991) *Situated Learning: Legitimate Peripheral Participation*, Cambridge University Press, Cambridge.

Lawn, M. (1986) Review of Ivor Goodson (ed.) *Social Histories of the Secondary Curriculum*, *History of Education*, 15/3, pp. 226–27.

Lawn, M. (1996) *Modern Times*, Falmer, London.

Lawn, M. and Furlong, J. (2009) 'The disciplines of education in the UK: between the ghost and the shadow', *Oxford Review of Education*, 35/5, pp. 541–52.

Lawn, M. and Grosvenor, I. (2007) '"When in doubt, preserve": exploring the traces of teaching and material culture in English schools', *History of Education*, 30/2, pp. 117–27.

Layton, D. (1973) *Science for the People: The Origins of the School Science Curriculum in England*, Allen and Unwin, London.

Layton, D. (1984) *Interpreters of Science: A History of the Association for Science Education*, London, Murray /ASE.

Leach, A. (1917) Some Results of Research in the History of Education in England with Suggestions for Its Continuance and Extension, British Academy, London (lecture presented 25 November 1914).

Leon, A. (1985) *The History of Education Today*, UNESCO, Paris.

Levin, R.A. (2000) 'After the fall: can historical studies return to faculties of education?', *Historical Studies in Education*, 12/1–2, pp. 155–62.

Levy, A. (2004) *Small Island*, London, Review.

Lindemann, B. (2000) 'History and educational reform', *Reviews in American History*, 28/1, pp. 142–50.

Lindmark, D., Erixon, P. and Simon, F. (eds) (2008) special issue, 'Technologies of the word: literacies in the history of education', *Paedagogica Historica*, 44/1–2.

Louis, W. (ed.) (1999) *The Oxford History of the British Empire* (5 volumes), Oxford University Press, Oxford.

Lowe, R. (ed.) (1983) *Trends in the Study and Teaching of the History of Education*, History of Education Society, Occasional Publication no 7, Leicester.

Lowe, R. (ed.) (2000) *History of Education: Major Themes* (4 volumes), Routledge, London.

Lowe, R. (2002) 'Do we still need history of education: Is it central or peripheral?', *History of Education*, 31/6, pp. 491–504.

Lowndes, G.A.N. (1937/1969) *The Silent Social Revolution: An Account of the Expansion of Public Education in England and Wales 1895–1965*, second edition, Oxford University Press, Oxford.

Lukes, S. (1973) *Emile Durkheim: His Life and Work*, Allen Lane, London.

Lupton, R. and Heath, N. (2008) *'A Failed Generation'? A Response to Michael Gove*, Institute of Education, London.

Luth, C. (2000) 'The International Standing Conference for the History of Education (1979–2000)' (paper downloaded from ISCHE website, http://www.ische.org, 12 June 2010).

McCulloch, G. (1982) 'Science education and the historiography of national decline', *Bulletin* of the History of Education Society, no 30, autumn, pp. 48–52.

McCulloch, G. (1986a) *Education in the Forming of New Zealand Society: Needs and Opportunities for Study*, New Zealand Association for Research in Education, Wellington.

McCulloch, G. (1986b) '"Secondary education without selection"? School zoning policy in Auckland since 1945', *New Zealand Journal of Educational Studies*, 21/2, pp. 98–112.

McCulloch, G. (1987) 'Curriculum history in England and New Zealand', in I. Goodson (ed.) *International Perspectives in Curriculum History*, Falmer, London, pp. 292–327.

McCulloch, G. (1988) 'From Currie to Picot: History, ideology and policy in New Zealand education', *Access*, 7, pp. 1–15.

McCulloch, G. (1989) *The Secondary Technical School: A Usable Past?* Falmer, London.

McCulloch, G. (1990) review of Bailey, *A Documentary History of New Zealand Education*, *Paedagogica Historica*, 26/1, pp. 117–22.

McCulloch, G. (1991) *Philosophers and Kings: Education for Leadership in Modern England*, Cambridge University Press, Cambridge.

McCulloch, G. (1994a) *Educational Reconstruction: The 1944 Education Act and the 21st Century*, Woburn, London.

McCulloch, G. (1994b) review of R. Openshaw, G. Lee and H. Lee, *Challenging the Myths*, *History of Education*, 23/3, pp. 317–19.

McCulloch, G. (1995a) 'Lessons from the class of 1944? History as education', in Peter Gordon (ed.) *The Study of Education: Inaugural Lectures*, volume 4, 'End of an era?', Woburn, London, pp. 249–68.

McCulloch, G. (1995b) 'Educational reconstruction: From the 1944 Education Act to the 21st century', inaugural lecture, University of Sheffield, 1 February.

McCulloch, G. (1997a) 'Privatising the past? History and education policy', *British Journal of Educational Studies*, 45/1, pp. 69–82.

McCulloch, G. (1997b) 'Marketing the millennium: Education for the twenty-first century', in R. Evans and A. Hargreaves (eds) *Beyond Educational Reform*, Open University Press, Buckingham, pp. 19–28.

McCulloch, G. (1998a) *Failing the Ordinary Child? The Theory and Practice of Working Class Secondary Education*, Open University Press, Buckingham.

McCulloch, G. (1998b) 'Historical studies in science education', *Studies in Science Education*, 31, pp. 31–54.

McCulloch, G. (2000) 'Publicising the educational past', in D. Crook and R. Aldrich (eds) *History of Education for the Twenty-First Century*, Institute of Education, London, pp. 1–16.

McCulloch, G. (2001) 'The reinvention of teacher professionalism', in R. Phillips and J. Furlong (eds) *Education, Reform and the State: Twenty-five Years of Politics, Policy and Practice*, RoutledgeFalmer, London, pp. 103–17.

McCulloch, G. (2002) '"Disciplines contributing to education"? Educational studies and the disciplines', *British Journal of Educational Studies*, 50/1, pp. 100–119.

McCulloch, G. (2003) 'Towards a social history of educational research', in J. Nixon, P. Sikes, W. Carr (eds) *The Moral Foundations of Educational Research: Knowledge, Inquiry and Values*, Open University Press, Maidenhead, pp. 18–31.

McCulloch, G. (2003b) 'Virtual history and the history of education', *History of Education*, 32/2, pp. 145–56.

McCulloch, G. (2004a) *Education, History and Social Change: The Legacy of Brian Simon*, Institute of Education, London.

McCulloch, G. (2004b) *Documentary Research in Education, History and the Social Sciences*, Routledge, London.

McCulloch, G. (2004c) 'I'm a teacher, get me back into here: student teachers in memory and history', *Journal of Educational Administration and History*, 36/2, pp. 179–85

McCulloch, G. (ed.) (2005a) *The RoutledgeFalmer Reader in the History of Education*, RoutledgeFalmer, London.

McCulloch, G. (2005b) 'Historical approaches to education and social change', *History of Education Researcher*, 75, pp. 4–7.

McCulloch, G. (2006) 'Education and the middle classes: the case of the English grammar schools, 1868–1944', *History of Education*, 35/6, pp. 689–704.

McCulloch, G. (2007a) *Cyril Norwood and the Ideal of Secondary Education*, Palgrave Macmillan, New York.

McCulloch, G. (2007b) 'National security and the history of education', in D. Crook and G. McCulloch (eds) *History, Politics and Policy-Making in Education*, Institute of Education, London, pp. 181–96.

McCulloch, G. (2007c) 'Forty years on', *History of Education*, 36/1, pp. 1–15.

McCulloch, G. (2008) 'Parity and prestige in English secondary education revisited', *British Journal of Sociology of Education*, 29/4, pp. 381–89.

McCulloch, G. (2009a) 'Empires and education: the British Empire', in R. Cowen and A. Kazamias (eds) *Handbook of Comparative Education*, Dordrecht, Springer, volume I, pp. 169–79.

McCulloch, G. (2009b) 'Putting the English middle class in its place: James Bryce and the Taunton commission, 1865–68', paper presented to the History of Education Society annual conference, Sheffield, December.

McCulloch, G. (2009c) 'The moral universe of Mr Chips: veteran teachers in British literature and drama', *Teachers and Teaching*, 15/4, pp. 409–20.

McCulloch, G. (2010) 'A people's history of education: Brian Simon, the British Communist Party, and *Studies in the History of Education, 1780–1870*', *History of Education*, 39/4, pp. 437–57.

McCulloch, G. (2011 in press) 'Historical and documentary research in education', in K. Morrison (ed.) *Research Methods in Education*, seventh edition, Routledge, London.

McCulloch, G., Layton, D. and Jenkins, E.W. (1985) *Technological Revolution? The Politics of School Science and Technology in England and Wales since 1945*, Falmer Press, London.

McCulloch, G. and Lowe, R. (eds) (2003) special issue, 'Centre and periphery: networks, space and geography in the history of education', *History of Education*.

McCulloch, G. and Richardson, W. (2000) *Historical Research in Educational Settings*, Open University Press, Buckingham.

McCulloch, G. and Watts, R. (2003) 'Introduction: Theory, methodology, and the history of education', *History of Education*, 32/2, pp. 129–32.

McCulloch, G., Goodman, J. and Richardson, W. (2005) 'Social change in the history of education: an ESRC seminar series', *History of Education Researcher*, 75, pp. 1–3.

McCulloch, G. and Woodin, T. (2010a) 'Towards a social history of learners and learning', *Oxford Review of Education*, 36/2, pp. 133–40.

McCulloch, G. and Woodin, T. (2010b) 'Learning and liberal education: the case of the Simon family, 1912–39', *Oxford Review of Education*, 36/2, pp. 187–201.

McCulloch, G. and Woodin, T. (eds) (2010c) special issue, 'Histories of learning in the modern world', *Oxford Review of Education*, 36/2.

McKenzie, D. (1984) 'Ideology and history of education in New Zealand', *New Zealand Journal of Educational Studies*, 19/1, pp. 2–9.

MacKenzie, J.W. (ed.) (1986) *Imperialism and Popular Culture*, Manchester University Press, Manchester.

MacKenzie, J.W. (1999a) 'Empire and metropolitan cultures', in A. Porter (ed.) *The Oxford History of the British Empire*, volume III, The Nineteenth Century, Oxford University Press, Oxford, pp. 270–93.

MacKenzie, J.W. (1999b) 'The popular culture of Empire in Britain', in J. Brown (ed.) *The Oxford History of the British Empire*, volume IV, The Twentieth Century, Oxford University Press, Oxford, pp. 212–31.

Mackinnon, A. (1984) 'Women's education: linking history and theory', *History of Education Review*, 13/2, pp. 5–14.

McLennan, G. (1981) *Marxism and the Methodologies of History*, NLB, London.

McMahon, J. (1995) 'ANZHES: the first twenty-five years' (paper downloaded from ANZHES website, 12 June 2010).

MacMillan, M. (2009) *The Uses and Abuses of History*, Profile Books, London.

Majorek, C., Johanningmeier, E.V., and Simon, F. (eds) (1998) *Schooling in Changing Societies: Historical and Comparative Perspectives.*, *Paedagogica Historica*, supplementary series, volume IV.

Mangan, J.A. (1978) 'Eton in India: the imperial diffusion of a Victorian educational ethic', *History of Education*, 7/2, pp. 105–18.

Mangan, J.A. (1986) *The Games Ethic and Imperialism: Aspects of the Diffusion of an Ideal*, Viking, London.

Mangan, J.A. (ed.) (1988) *'Benefits Bestowed'? Education and British Imperialism*, Manchester University Press, Manchester.

Mangan, J.A. (ed.) (1993) *The Imperial Curriculum: Racial Images and Education in the British Colonial Experience*, Routledge, London.

Mangan, J.A. and Walvin, J. (eds) (1987) *Manliness and Morality: Middle-class Masculinity in Britain and America, 1800–1940*, Manchester University Press, Manchester.

Margolis, E. and Rowe, J. (2004) 'Images of assimilation: photographs of Indian schools in Arizona', *History of Education*, 332/2, pp. 199–230.

Marsden, W.E. (ed.) (1979) *Post-War Curriculum Development: An Historical Appraisal*, History of Education Society, Leicester.

Marshall, J. and Peters, M. (1990) 'The insertion of "New Right" thinking into education: an example from New Zealand', *Journal of Education Policy*, 5/2, pp. 143–56.

Martin, J. (2003) 'The hope of biography: the historical recovery of women educator activists', *History of Education*, 32/2, pp. 219–32.

Martin, J. (2007) 'Thinking education histories differently: biographical approaches to class politics and women's movements in London, 1900s to 1960s', *History of Education*, 36/4–5, pp. 315–33.

Maton, K. (ed.) (2010) *Social Realism, Knowledge and the Sociology of Education: Coalitions of the Mind*, Continuum, London.

Maud, J. (1952) 'The twentieth-century administrator', in A.V. Judges (ed.) *Pioneers of English Education*, pp. 227–47.

May, J. (2008) '*Puberty Blues* and the representation of an Australian comprehensive high school', *History of Education Review*, 37/2, pp. 61–67.

Miller, P. (1989) 'Education and the state: the uses of Marxist and feminist approaches to the writing of histories of schooling', *Historical Studies in Education*, 1/2, pp. 285–303.

Mills, C.W. (1959) *The Sociological Imagination*, Oxford University Press, London.

Montgomery, L.M. (1908/2004) *Anne of Green Gables*, Broadview Press, Peterborough, Ontario.

Montgomery, L.M. (1925/1994) *Anne of Avonlea*, Penguin, London.

Morris, P. (1952) 'The English tradition of education', in A.V. Judges (ed.) *Pioneers of English Education*, pp. 42–63.

Muller, D., Ringer, F. and Simon, B. (eds) (1987) *The Rise of the Modern Educational System: Structural Change and Social Transformation 1870–1920*, Cambridge University Press, Cambridge.

Murphy, R. (1996) 'Like a bridge over troubled water: realizing the potential of educational research', *British Educational Research Journal*, 22/1, pp. 3–15.

Musgrave, P. (1970) 'A model for the analysis of the development of the English educational system from 1860', in P.W. Musgrave (ed.) *Sociology, History and Education: A Reader*, Methuen, London, pp. 15–29.

Myers, K. (1999) 'National identity, citizenship and education for displacement: Spanish refugee children in Cambridge, 1937' *History of Education*, 28/3, pp. 313–25.

Myers, K. (2001) 'The hidden history of refugee schooling: the case of the Belgians, 1914–18', *History of Education*, 30/2, pp. 153–62.

Myers, K. (2009) 'Immigrants and ethnic minorities in the history of education', *Paedagogica Historica*, 45/6, pp. 801–16.

Myers, K., Grosvenor, I. and Watts, R. (eds) (2008) special issue, 'Education and globalisation', *History of Education*, 37/6.

Nash, M.A. (2008) 'The historiography of education for girls and women in the United States', in W. Reese and J. Rury (eds) *Rethinking the History of American Education*, pp. 143–59.

Nunn, P. (1937) letter to Fred Clarke, 5 January (Clarke papers, Institute of Education, University of London, file 38).

Obelkevich, J. (2000) 'New developments in history in the 1950s and 1960s', *Contemporary British History*, 14/4, pp. 128–42.

O'Donoghue, T. and Potts, A. (2004) 'Researching the lives of Catholic teachers who were members of religious orders: historiographical considerations', *History of Education*, 33/4, pp. 469–81.

Oliphant, J. (2006) 'Empowerment and debilitation in the educational experience of the blind in nineteenth-century England and Scotland', *History of Education*, 35/1, pp. 47–68.

Olneck, M.R. (2008) 'American public schooling and European immigrants in the early twentieth century: a post-revisionist synthesis', in W. Reese and J. Rury (eds) *Rethinking the History of American Education*, pp. 103–41.

Olssen, M. (1987) 'What really happened? Varieties of educational history', in R. Openshaw and D. McKenzie (eds) *Reinterpreting the Educational Past*, pp. 21–38.

Openshaw, R. (1987) 'Introduction', in R. Openshaw and D. McKenzie (eds) *Reinterpreting the Educational Past*, pp. 1–7.

Openshaw, R. (2009) *Reforming New Zealand Secondary Education: The Picot Report and the Road to Radical Reform*, PalgraveMacmillan, New York.

Openshaw, R., Lee, G., Lee, H. (1993) *Challenging the Myths: Rethinking New Zealand's Educational History*, Dunmore Press, Palmerston North.

Openshaw, R., McKenzie, D. (eds) (1987) *Reinterpreting the Educational Past: Essays in the History of New Zealand Education*, New Zealand Council of Educational Research, Wellington.

Osborne, G. (2007) Reaction: UN report on child wellbeing, *Society Guardian*, 14 February (http://www.guardian.co.uk; last accessed 1 November 2010).

Paedagogica Historica (1961) Editorial, 1/1, p. 4.

Pelling, H. (1958) *The British Communist Party: A Historical Profile*, George Allen and Unwin, London.

Perkin, H. (1989) *The Rise of Professional Society: England since 1800*, Routledge, London.

Peters, R.S. (1963/1980) 'Education as initiation', in P. Gordon (ed.) *The Study of Education*, volume 1, Woburn, London, pp. 273–99.

Petersen, R.C. (1992) *History of Education Research: What it is and how to do it*, NTU Printing, Sydney.

Pollock, L. (1990) *Forgotten Children: Parent-Child Relations from 1500 to 1900*, Cambridge University Press, Cambridge.

Popkewitz, T., Franklin, B., Pereyra, M. (eds) (2001) *Cultural History and Education: Critical Essays on Knowledge and Schooling*, RoutledgeFalmer, London.

Popkewitz, T., Pereyra, M., Franklin, B. (2001) 'History, the problem of knowledge, and the new cultural history of schooling', in T. Popkewitz, B. Franklin, M. Pereyra (eds), *Cultural History and Education*, pp. 3–42.

Power, S., Edwards, T., Whitty, G., Wigfall, V. (2003) *Education and the Middle Class*, Open University Press, Buckingham.

Pritchard, D.C. (1963) *Education and the Handicapped, 1760–1960*, Routledge and Kegan Paul, London.

Purvis, J. (1980) 'Working class women and adult education in nineteenth-century Britain', *History of Education*, 9/3, pp. 193–212.

Purvis, J. (1989) *Hard Lessons: The Lives and Education of Working-Class Women in Nineteenth-Century England*, Polity Press, Cambridge.

Purvis, J. (1992) 'The historiography of British education: a feminist critique', in A. Rattansi and D. Reeder (eds) *Rethinking Radical Education: Essays in Honour of Brian Simon*, Lawrence and Wishart, London, pp. 249–66.

Quick, R.H. (1868/1902) *Essays on Educational Reformers*, Longmans Green, London.

Race, R. (2004) 'Core or periphery? The past and present of the history of education', *British Educational Research Journal*, 30/2, pp. 313–24.

Raffe, D. and Spours, K. (eds) (2007) *Policy-making and Policy Learning in 14–19 Education*, Bedford Way Papers, Institute of Education, London.

Raftery, D., McDermid, J., and Jones, G.E. (2007) 'Social change and education in Ireland, Scotland and Wales: historiography on nineteenth-century schooling', *History of Education*, 36/4–5, pp. 447–63.

Randall, P. (1987) 'The position of the history of education in South African universities', *History of Education Society Bulletin*, 44, pp. 51–55.

Rattansi, A. and Reeder, D. (1992) 'Introduction', in A. Rattansi and D. Reeder (eds) *Rethinking Radical Education: Essays in Honour of Brian Simon*, Lawrence and Wishart, London, pp. 7–24.

Ravitch, D. (1978) *The Revisionists Revised: A Critique of the Radical Attack on the Schools*, Basic Books, New York.

Reese, W. and Rury, J. (eds) (2008a) *Rethinking the History of American Education*, Palgrave Macmillan, New York.

Reese, W. and Rury, J. (2008b) 'Introduction: An evolving and expanding field of study', in W. Reese and J. Rury (eds) *Rethinking the History of American Education*, pp. 1–16.

Reese, W. and Rury, J. (2008c) 'Epilogue: New directions in the history of education', in W. Reese and J. Rury (eds) *Rethinking the History of American Education*, pp. 281–85.

Reeves, W.P. (1898) *The Long White Cloud: Ao Tea Roa*, Wellington, H. Marshall.

Reid. W.A. (1986) 'Curriculum theory and curriculum change: what can we learn from history?', in P.H. Taylor (ed.) *Recent Developments in Curriculum Studies*, NFER-Nelson, Windsor, pp. 75–83.

Reisz, M. (2009) 'Through the myths of time', *Times Higher Education*, 28 May.

Renwick, W.L. (1986) unpublished referee's report on article for *New Zealand Journal of Educational Studies*, 24 April.

Research Assessment Exercise (2008) Sub-Panel 45 Education subject overview report, (http://www.rae.ac.uk/pubs/2009/ov/; last accessed 1 November 2010).

Richardson, W. (1999) 'Historians and educationists: the history of education as a field of study', Part I, 1945–72, *History of Education*, 28/1, pp. 1–30; Part II, 1972–96, *History of Education*, 28/2, pp. 109–41.

Robinson, W. (2000) 'Finding our professional niche: reinventing ourselves as twenty-first century historians of education', in D. Crook and R. Aldrich (eds) *History of Education for the Twenty-First Century*, pp. 50–62.

Robinson, W. (2004) *Power to Teach: Learning through Practice*, Woburn, London.

Rosario, J. (2007) 'Soul making in the comprehensive high school: the legacies of Frederick Wiseman's *High School* and *High School II*', in B.M. Franklin and G. McCulloch (eds) *The Death of the Comprehensive High School? Historical, Contemporary, and Comparative Perspectives*, Palgrave Macmillan, New York, pp. 93–109.

Rose, J. (2001) *The Intellectual Life of the British Working Classes*, Yale University Press, London.

Rose, J. (2007) 'The history of education as the history of reading', *History of Education*, 36/4–5, pp. 595–605

Rousmaniere, K. (1997) *City Teachers: Teaching and School Reform in Historical Perspective*, Teachers College Press, New York.

Rousmaniere, K. (2009) 'The great divide: principals, teachers, and the long hallway between them', *History of Education Review*, 38/2, pp. 17–27.

Rury, J. (2006) 'The curious status of the history of education: a parallel perspective', *History of Education Quarterly*, 46/4, pp. 571–98.

Said, E.W. (1994) *Culture and Imperialism*, Verso, London.

Salimova, K. and Dodde, N. (eds) (2000) *International Handbook on History of Education*, Orbita-M., Moscow.

Salimova, K. and Johanningmeier. E. (eds) (1993) *Why Should We Teach the History of Education?* International Academy of Self-Improvement, Moscow.

Samuel, R. (ed.) (1981) *People's History and Socialist Theory*, Routledge and Kegan Paul, London.

Samuel, R. (1998) *Theatres of Memory*, volume II, Island Stories, Unravelling Britain, London, Verso.

Scott, D. (2000) *Realism and Educational Research: New Perspectives and Possibilities*, London, Routledge.

Searby, P. (ed.) (1982) *Educating the Victorian Middle Class*, History of Education Society, Leicester.

Seldon, A. (2010) 'Commentary', *The Observer*, 14 February.

Sharp, R. and Green, A. (1975) *Education and Social Control: A Study in Progressive Primary Education*. Routledge and Kegan Paul, London.

Shor, I. (1986) *Culture Wars: School and Society in the Conservative Restoration, 1964–1984*, RKP, London.

Shuker, R. (1980a) 'Review: "History of State Education in New Zealand: 1840–1975"', *Delta*, no 26, June, pp. 37–39.

Shuker, R. (1980b) 'New Zealand's educational history: a revisionist perspective?', *Delta*, 27, November, pp. 38–47.

Shuker, R. (1986) 'The state, schooling and hegemony: education in New Zealand prior to 1930', *Sites: A Journal for Radical Perspectives on Culture*, 12, autumn, pp. 15–28.

Shuker, R. (1987) *The One Best System? A Revisionist History of State Schooling in New Zealand*, Dunmore Press, Palmerston North.

Silver, H. (1983) *Education as History: Interpreting Nineteenth- and Twentieth-Century Education*, Methuen, London.

Silver, H. (1986) 'Debunking the myths of a historical perspective', *Times Higher Education Supplement*, 26 December.

Silver, H. (1990) *Education, Change and the Policy Process*, London, Falmer.

Simon, B. (1937) essay, 'The function of the school in society' (Simon papers, Institute of Education, University of London: SIM/5/2/5).

Simon, B. (1946) 'The education campaign' (Communist Party circular, Lancashire and Cheshire District) (Simon papers: SIM/4/5/1/41).

Simon, B. (1949a) 'The comprehensive school', *Communist Review*, April, pp. 486–91.

Simon, B. (1949b) 'The theory and practice of intelligence testing', *Communist Review*, October, pp. 687–95.

Simon, B. (1955a) note, 'Education in the nineteenth century', 9 February (Simon papers, SIM/4/1/14).

Simon, B. (1955b) note, 'Synopsis: Education in the nineteenth century', 24 March (Simon papers, SIM/4/1/14)

Simon, B. (1960a) *Studies in the History of Education*, Lawrence and Wishart, London.

Simon, B. (1960b) note, 'Education and class struggle in history', February–March (Simon papers, SIM/4/2/3).

Simon, B. (1960c) note, 'History of education' (Simon papers, SIM/4/2/3).

Simon, B. (1961) note, 'Revised synopsis, Studies in the History of Education, 1870–1940', 21 March (Simon papers, SIM/4/2/8).

Simon, B. (1965) *Education and the Labour Movement, 1870–1920*, Lawrence and Wishart, London.

Simon, B. (1966) 'The history of education', in J.W. Tibble (ed.) *The Study of Education*, Routledge and Kegan Paul, London, pp. 91–131.

Simon, B. (1971) note, 'Chapter 4: Education, politics and society, 1920–40', 4 September (Simon papers, SIM/4/3/16).

Simon, B. (1974) *The Politics of Educational Reform, 1920–1940*, Lawrence and Wishart, London.

Simon, B. (1977) note, 'Volume 4', 14 September (Simon papers, SIM/4/4/74).

Simon, B. (1978) 'Educational research: which way?', *British Educational Research Journal*, 4/1, pp. 2–7.

Simon, B. (1985a) 'Can education change society?' In B. Simon, *Does Education Matter?* Lawrence and Wishart, London, pp. 13–31 (reprinted in McCulloch (ed.) (2005b), *The Routledge-Falmer Reader in the History of Education*, pp. 139–50)).

Simon, B. (1985b) diary, 27 January (Simon papers, SIM/4/4/46).

Simon, B. (1988) diary, 3 May (Simon papers, SIM/4/4/46).

Simon, B. (1989) 'Synopsis: Chapter 2 – The Labour Government in control, 1945–51' (Simon papers, SIM/4/4/14).

Simon, B. (1990) note, 'Random thoughts, 1940–80', 14 September (Simon papers, SIM/4/4/74).

Simon, B. (1991) *Education and the Social Order, 1940–1990*, Lawrence and Wishart, London.

Simon, B. (1992) 'The politics of comprehensive reorganisation: a retrospective analysis', *History of Education*, 21/4, pp. 355–62.

Simon, B. (1994) 'The history of education: its importance for understanding', in his *The State and Educational Change: Essays in the History of Education and Pedagogy*, Lawrence and Wishart, London, pp. 3–19.

Simon, B. (1997) 'A seismic change: process and interpretation', in R. Pring and G. Walford (eds) *Affirming the Comprehensive Ideal*, Falmer, London, pp. 13–28.

Simon, B. (1998) *A Life in Education*, Lawrence and Wishart, London.

Simon, B. (n.d. [1990s]) unpublished autobiography (Simon papers).

Simon, J. (1977) 'The history of education in *Past and Present*', *Oxford Review of Education*, 3/1, pp. 71–86.

Simon, J. (2007) 'An "energetic and controversial historian of education yesterday and today": A.F. Leach (1851–1915)', *History of Education*, 36/3, pp. 367–80.

Sinclair, K. (1961) *A History of New Zealand*, Oxford University Press, London.

Skidmore, C. (2008) *The Failed Generation: The Real Cost of Education under Labour*, Bow Group, London.

Skinningsrud, T. (2005) 'Realist social theories and the emergence of state educational systems', *Journal of Critical Realism*, 4/2, pp. 339–65.

Smith, M.M. (2007) *Sensory History*, Berg, Oxford.

Snow, C.P. (1959/1964) *The Two Cultures and a Second Look*, Cambridge University Press, Cambridge.

Spaull, A. (1981) 'Australian educational history', *History of Education Quarterly*, 21/4, pp. 501–8.

Spencer, S. (2007) '"Until our membership and funds build up": forty years of *The History of Education Society Bulletin/Researcher*', *History of Education Researcher*, no 79, May, pp. 47–51.

Spiegel, G. (ed.) (2005) *Practicing History: New Directions in Historical Writing after the Linguistic Turn*, Routledge, London.

Standish, P. (2008) 'Chroniclers and critics', *Paedagogica Historica*, 44/6, pp. 661–75.

Stedman Jones, G. (1972) 'History: the poverty of empiricism', in R. Blackburn (ed.) *Ideology in Social Science: Readings in Critical Social Theory*, Fontana, London, pp. 96–115.

Steinmetz, G. (1998) 'Critical realism and historical sociology: a review article', *Comparative Studies in Society and History*, 40/1, pp. 170–86.

Steinmetz, G. (ed.) (2005) *The Politics of Method in the Human Sciences: Positivism and its Epistemological Others*, Duke University Press, London.

Stephens, W.B. (1989) Review essay, 'Primary education in postwar England', *History of Education Quarterly*, 29/1, pp. 451–54.

Stephenson, M. (2008) 'Timeless projects: remembering and voice in the history of education', *History of Education Review*, 37/2, pp. 3–13.

Stern, F. (1956a) 'Introduction', in F. Stern (ed.) *The Varieties of History from Voltaire to the Present*, pp. 11–32.

Stern, F. (ed.) (1956b) *The Varieties of History from Voltaire to the Present*, World Publishing Company, London.

Stocks, M. (1963) *Ernest Simon of Manchester*, Manchester University Press, Manchester.

Stone, L. (ed.) (1975) *The University in Society*, volume I, Princeton University Press, Princeton.

Stone, L. (ed.) (1976) *Schooling and Society: Studies in the History of Education*, Johns Hopkins University Press, Ballarat.

Stone, L. (1977) *The Family, Sex and Marriage in England 1500–1800*, Weidenfeld and Nicolson, London.

Stones, E. (1985) 'The development of the British Educational Research Association', *British Educational Research Journal*, 11/2, pp. 85–90.

Styles, M. (2010) 'Learning through literature: the case of *The Arabian Nights*', *Oxford Review of Education*, 36/2, pp. 157–69.

Sutherland, G. (1969) 'The study of the history of education', *History*, 59, pp. 49–59

Symonds, R. (1986) *Oxford and Empire; The Last Lost Cause?* Oxford University Press, Oxford.

Talbott, J.E. (1971) 'The history of education', *Daedalus*, 100/1, pp. 136–50.

Tamboukou, M. (2010) 'Narratives from within: an Arendtian approach to life histories and the writing of history', *Journal of Educational Administration and History*, 42/2, pp. 115–31.

Taskforce to review education administration (1988) *Administering for Excellence: Effective Administration in Education*, New Zealand Government, Wellington.

Tawney, R.H. (1914/1964) 'An experiment in radical education', in R. H. Tawney, *The Radical Tradition*, Penguin, London, pp. 74–85.

The Guardian (2009) report, 'Government working with Tory grandee on technical school revival', 31 August.

Theobald, M. (1988) 'The accomplished woman and the propriety of intellect: a new look at women's education in Britain and Australia, 1800–850', *History of Education*, 17/1, pp. 21–36.

The Times (1992), leading article, 'State knows best', 29 July.

The Times (2007) report, 'Outcry after Unicef identifies UK's "failed generation of children"', 14 February.

Thompson, W., Parker, D. Waite, M., Morgan, D. (eds) (1995) *Historiography and the British Marxist Historians*, Pluto Press, London.

Tibble, J.W. (ed.) (1966) *The Study of Education*, Routledge and Kegan Paul, London

Times Educational Supplement (1987) report, 'Dramatic steps that will carry Britain forward'.

Timutimu, N., Simon, J., Matthews, K. (1998) 'Historical research as a bicultural project: seeking new perspectives on the New Zealand Native Schools system', *History of Education*, 27/2, pp. 109–24.

Tooley, J. (1998) *Educational Research: A Critique*, Office for Standards in Education, London.

Trimingham Jack, C. (2009) 'Education and ambition in *Anne of Avonlea*', *History of Education Review*, 38/2, pp. 109–20.

Tropp, A. (1957) *The School Teachers: The Growth of the Teaching Profession in England and Wales from 1800 to the Present Day*, Heinemann, London.

Tyack, D. (1974) *The One Best System: A History of American Urban Education*, Harvard University Press, Cambridge, Mass.

Tyack, D. (1991) 'Public school reform: policy talk and institutional practice', *American Journal of Education*, 100/1, pp. 1–19.

Tyack, D. and Cuban, L. (1995) *Tinkering Toward Utopia: A Century of Public School Reform*, Harvard University Press, Cambridge, Mass.

Tyack, D., Lowe, R., and Hansot, E. (1984) *Public Schools in Hard Times: The Great Depression and Recent Years*, Harvard University Press, Cambridge Mass.

Tveit, K. (1990) 'The British prehistory of ISCHE', *History of Education Society Bulletin*, no 45, pp. 38–46.

UNICEF (2007) *Report Card 7: An Overview of Child Wellbeing in Rich Countries*, UNICEF, Paris.

Veblen, T. (1899/1973) *The Theory of the Leisure Class*, Houghton Mifflin Company, Boston.

Verstraete, P. (2009) 'Savage solitude: the problematisation of disability at the turn of the eighteenth century', *Paedagogica Historica*, 45/1, pp. 269–89.

Vick, M. (2009) 'Re-imagining teachers' work: photographs of Blackfriar's School, Sydney, 1913–23 as representations of an educational alternative', *History of Education Review*, 38/2, pp. 82–93.

Vincent, D. (2000) *The Rise of Mass Literacy: Reading and Writing in Modern Europe*, Polity Press, Cambridge.

Vincent, D. (2003) 'The progress of literacy', *Victorian Studies*, 45/3, pp. 405–31.

Vinovskis, M. (1999) *History and Educational Policy Making*, Yale University Press, New Haven.

Walker, R. (1983) Review of Ivor Goodson's *School Subjects and Curriculum Change*, *History of Education*, 12/4, pp. 312–13.

Walsh, P. (2008) 'Education and the "universalist" idiom of empire: Irish National School Books in Ireland and Ontario', *History of Education*, 37/5, pp. 645–60.

Waring, M. (1979) *Social Pressures and Curriculum Innovation: A Study of the Nuffield Foundation Science Teaching Project*, Methuen, London.

Warren, D. (1978) 'A past for the present', in Donald Warren (ed.) *History, Education, and Public Policy: Recovering the American Educational Past*, McCutchan, Berkeley, pp. 1–20.

Watts, R. (2005) 'Gendering the story: change in the history of education', *History of Education*, 34/3, pp. 225–41.

Watts, R. (2007) 'Whose knowledge? Gender, education, science and history', *History of Education*, 36/3, pp. 283–302.

Watts, R. (2009) 'Education, empire and social change in nineteenth century England', *Paedagogica Historica*, 45/6, pp. 773–86.

Weber, S. and Mitchell, C. (1995) *'That's Funny, You Don't Look Like a Teacher': Interrogating Image and Identity in Popular Culture*, RoutledgeFalmer, London.

Webster, C. (1976) 'Changing perspectives in the history of education', *Oxford Review of Education*, 2/3, pp. 201–13.

Weiler, K. and Middleton, S. (eds) (1999) *Telling Women's Lives: Narrative Inquiries in the History of Women's Education*, Open University Press, Buckingham.

Wenger, E. (1998) *Communities of Practice: Learning, Meaning, and Identity*, Cambridge University Press, Cambridge.

White, C. (2003) 'Historicizing educational disparity: colonial policy and Fijian educational attainment', *History of Education*, 32/4, pp. 345–65.

Whitehead, C. (1988) 'British colonial educational policy: a synonym for cultural imperialism?', in J.A. Mangan (ed.) *'Benefits Bestowed?'*, pp. 211–30.

Whitehead, C. (2003) *Colonial Educators: The British Indian and Colonial Education Service, 1858–1983*, I.B. Tauris, London.

Whitehead, K. (2010) '"A decided disadvantage for the kindergarten students to mix with the state teachers"', *Paedagogica Historica*, 46/1–2, pp. 85–97.

Whitty, G. (2006) 'Education(al) research and education policy making: is conflict inevitable?', *British Educational Research Journal*, 32/2, pp. 159–76.

Williams, R. (1958) *Culture and Society, 1780–1950*, Chatto and Windus, London.

Williams, R. (1961) *The Long Revolution*, Chatto and Windus, London.

Wilson, J.D. (1984) 'From social control to family strategies: some observations on recent trends in Canadian educational history', *History of Education Review*, 13/1, pp. 1–13.

Woodin, T. (2005) 'Muddying the waters: class and identity in a working class cultural organisation', *Sociology*, 39/5, pp. 1001–18.

Woodin, T. (2007) 'Working class education and social change in nineteenth- and twentieth-century Britain', *History of Education*, 36/4–5, pp. 483–96.

Wright, S. (2009) 'The work of teachers and others in and around a Birmingham slum school 1891–1920', *History of Education*, 38/6, pp. 729–46.

Young, M. (1958) *The Rise of the Meritocracy: An Essay on Education and Equality*, Chatto and Windus, London.

Young, M.F.D. (ed.) (1971a) *Knowledge and Control: New Directions for the Sociology of Education*, Collier-Macmillan, London

Young, M.F.D. (1971b) 'An approach to the study of curricula as socially organised knowledge', in M.F.D. Young (ed.) *Knowledge and Control*, pp. 19–46

Young, M.F.D. (1976) 'The schooling of science', in M. Young and G. Whitty (eds) *Explorations in the Politics of School Knowledge*, Driffield, Nafferton Books, pp. 47–61.

Young, M.F.D. (2008) *Bringing Knowledge Back In: From Social Constructivism to Social Realism in the Sociology of Education*, Routledge, London.

Zoller, M. (2003) 'Settler, missionary, and the State: contradictions in the formulation of educational policy in colonial Swaziland', *History of Education*, 32/1, pp. 35–56.

Index